Living with Quiet Borderline Personality Disorder

The Complete Guide for Families, Partners, and Those Who Love Someone with High-Functioning BPD

Kimberly Daisy Paper

Table of Contents

Chapter 1: The Hidden Face of BPD

Research indicates that approximately 75% of individuals with borderline personality disorder exhibit what clinicians term *internalizing presentations*—symptoms that turn inward rather than manifesting as external, observable behaviors (Carpenter et al., 2013). This phenomenon challenges traditional diagnostic frameworks and leaves millions of people struggling with intense emotional dysregulation while appearing perfectly functional to the outside world. Unlike the classic presentation of BPD characterized by dramatic interpersonal conflicts and visible self-destructive behaviors, quiet BPD operates beneath the surface, creating a unique clinical picture that mental health professionals are only beginning to understand.

The internalizing nature of quiet BPD creates what researchers call a *diagnostic shadow*—a space where significant psychological distress exists without meeting conventional criteria for identification (Paris, 2019). This population demonstrates the same core features of emotional instability, identity disturbance, and interpersonal difficulties as those with classic BPD presentations, but these symptoms manifest through self-criticism, emotional suppression, and internal chaos rather than external acting out.

What Makes Quiet BPD Different from Classic BPD

Traditional borderline personality disorder presents with what mental health professionals recognize as *externalizing behaviors*—actions directed outward that others can observe and identify. These include dramatic relationship conflicts, public emotional outbursts, visible self-harm, impulsive spending or sexual behavior, and overt threats of abandonment. The individual with classic BPD makes their distress known, often in ways that demand immediate attention and intervention.

Quiet BPD operates through *internalizing mechanisms* that direct the same intense emotions inward (Zanarini et al., 2018). Instead of screaming at a partner during conflict, the person with quiet BPD engages in harsh self-criticism and emotional withdrawal. Rather than threatening suicide openly, they experience persistent suicidal ideation while maintaining their daily responsibilities. The fear of abandonment becomes a constant internal vigilance rather than desperate clinging behaviors that others can see.

The core difference lies in *emotional expression patterns*. Classic BPD involves emotional dysregulation that spills outward, affecting everyone in the person's environment. Quiet BPD contains this dysregulation internally, creating what appears to be emotional stability while the individual experiences the same intensity of feeling. This containment requires enormous psychological energy and often leads to what clinicians observe as *high-functioning depression*—the ability to perform tasks and maintain relationships while suffering significantly.

Emotional processing also differs fundamentally between presentations. Classic BPD typically involves rapid cycling between emotional extremes with external expression of each state. Quiet BPD demonstrates the same emotional intensity but processes these feelings through rumination, self-blame, and internal analysis. A perceived rejection might trigger hours of internal questioning and self-attack rather than an immediate confrontation with the person involved.

The *interpersonal style* varies considerably as well. Classic BPD often involves tumultuous relationships with frequent breakups, dramatic reconciliations, and intense conflicts. Quiet BPD relationships appear stable on the surface but involve significant internal turmoil. The individual may maintain long-term relationships while experiencing constant fear of abandonment, analyzing every interaction for signs of rejection, and engaging in extensive people-pleasing behaviors to prevent perceived threats to the relationship.

Self-harm behaviors in quiet BPD tend toward emotional rather than physical expressions. While classic BPD might involve cutting, burning, or other visible forms of self-injury, quiet BPD manifests through emotional self-harm such as harsh internal criticism, self-sabotage of achievements, and deliberate denial of personal needs or pleasures. This emotional self-punishment can be just as damaging but remains invisible to others.

Why Traditional Resources Miss This Population

Mental health resources have historically focused on crisis intervention and behaviors that disrupt social functioning (Linehan, 2014). The development of dialectical behavior therapy (DBT), the gold standard treatment for BPD, emerged from work with individuals who exhibited severe self-harm behaviors and frequent hospitalizations. While these interventions prove effective for quiet BPD, the assessment tools and screening procedures often fail to identify internalized presentations.

Diagnostic criteria create systemic blind spots. The DSM-5 criteria for borderline personality disorder emphasize observable behaviors and interpersonal dysfunction. Criteria such as "frantic efforts to avoid real or imagined abandonment" typically manifest as visible clingy or demanding behavior in classic presentations. In quiet BPD, these same efforts occur internally through hypervigilance, excessive reassurance-seeking disguised as normal conversation, and preemptive emotional withdrawal that appears as independence.

Screening instruments used in clinical settings often miss quiet BPD presentations because they focus on external behaviors and crisis situations. Standard questions about self-harm ask about cutting or burning rather than emotional self-punishment. Inquiries about relationship problems focus on breakups and conflicts rather than internal relationship anxiety and people-pleasing patterns. Assessment tools for suicidal ideation emphasize plans and intent rather than chronic passive death wishes that characterize many quiet BPD experiences.

Training gaps in mental health education contribute to underrecognition. Most clinical training programs emphasize crisis management and severe presentations because these cases require immediate intervention. Students learn to identify and treat the individuals who end up in emergency rooms and crisis units. The person with quiet BPD who maintains employment, pays bills on time, and avoids hospitalization receives less attention in training curricula.

The *therapeutic relationship* itself can mask quiet BPD presentations. These individuals often present as ideal clients—motivated, insightful, and compliant with treatment recommendations. They may receive diagnoses of anxiety or depression without deeper exploration of identity issues, emotional intensity, and interpersonal patterns that characterize borderline presentations. The pleasing nature of their therapeutic presentation can prevent clinicians from recognizing the underlying personality organization.

Cultural factors also contribute to underrecognition. Societies that value emotional control and individual achievement may inadvertently reinforce quiet BPD presentations. The ability to function despite internal distress becomes a source of pride rather than a signal for help. Family systems that emphasize appearance and success over emotional expression may produce individuals who learn early to internalize their struggles.

Research funding and clinical attention naturally flow toward presentations that create immediate safety concerns or social disruption. Quiet BPD, by definition, doesn't create the same urgency for intervention. This creates a cycle where resources remain focused on externalizing presentations while internalizing ones receive less study and fewer targeted interventions.

The High-Functioning Mask and Internal Chaos

The hallmark of quiet BPD lies in the profound disconnect between external presentation and internal experience. Clinical observations reveal that individuals with this presentation often achieve significant external success while experiencing severe internal distress (Kreisman & Straus, 2010). They may excel in their careers, maintain long-term relationships, and appear to have their lives together while struggling with the same emotional intensity and identity confusion that characterizes all BPD presentations.

Performance-based identity formation characterizes much of the quiet BPD experience. These individuals often develop a sense of self based entirely on external achievements and others' approval. A successful professional presentation may mask complete uncertainty about personal values, desires, and authentic identity. The performance becomes so convincing that even close family members may not recognize the internal struggle.

Perfectionism serves as both a coping mechanism and a source of distress. The drive for flawless performance protects against perceived criticism or abandonment but creates impossible standards that guarantee frequent feelings of failure. A minor work mistake might trigger hours of internal self-attack, while external observers see only someone who consistently delivers high-quality results. This perfectionism often extends to emotional expression—the person with quiet BPD may feel they must always appear positive and capable, adding emotional suppression to their internal burden.

The internal experience involves constant emotional monitoring and regulation. These individuals become experts at reading social cues and adjusting their behavior to maintain approval and avoid conflict. This hypervigilance creates exhaustion that others cannot see. A simple social interaction may trigger extensive internal analysis: "Did they seem less friendly than usual? Did I say something wrong? Are they pulling away from me?" This internal dialogue continues long after the interaction ends.

Emotional intensity remains just as severe as in classic BPD presentations but gets channeled into internal experiences rather than external expression. A perceived slight might trigger the same rage response as in classic BPD, but instead of yelling or acting out, the person with quiet BPD experiences this rage as intense self-criticism or emotional shutdown. The energy that would go into external conflict becomes turned inward, creating depression, anxiety, and somatic symptoms.

Dissociation and emotional numbing frequently occur as protective mechanisms against overwhelming internal states. When emotions become too intense to process, the individual may experience periods of feeling disconnected from themselves or their surroundings. This can manifest as going through the motions of daily life while feeling emotionally absent, or experiencing periods where emotions feel completely shut down. Others may notice subtle signs—seeming distracted or "not quite present"—but the full extent of the internal experience remains hidden.

The *physical toll* of maintaining this high-functioning facade often manifests as chronic fatigue, frequent illness, sleep disturbances, and stress-related health problems. The energy required to constantly monitor and regulate emotions while maintaining external performance depletes physical resources. Many individuals with quiet BPD report feeling exhausted despite appearing capable and energetic to others.

Clinical Recognition and Internal Experience

Understanding quiet BPD requires recognizing the sophisticated defense mechanisms that maintain external functioning while protecting against core vulnerabilities. These individuals often develop what clinicians term *functional dissociation*—the ability to compartmentalize emotional experiences to maintain performance in specific life areas (Herman, 2015). A person might experience intense suicidal ideation in the morning but deliver an effective presentation at work in the afternoon, with neither experience invalidating the other.

Emotional regulation strategies in quiet BPD tend toward overcontrol rather than undercontrol. While classic BPD involves emotional expression that feels uncontrollable, quiet BPD involves such tight emotional control that spontaneous emotional expression becomes extremely difficult. This overcontrol can be just as problematic as undercontrol, leading to emotional constipation, depression, and disconnection from authentic feelings.

Interpersonal relationships reflect this same pattern of overcontrol and internal monitoring. The person with quiet BPD may rarely express needs directly, instead hoping others will intuitively understand their requirements. They often become expert caretakers of others' emotions while neglecting their own emotional needs. Conflict avoidance becomes a primary strategy, sometimes to the detriment of authentic relationship connection.

Identity disturbance in quiet BPD often manifests as feeling like a chameleon—constantly adapting to meet others' expectations without a clear sense of authentic self. This may not be immediately apparent because the adaptations often involve taking on socially valued traits like helpfulness, competence, or agreeableness. The individual may be seen as stable and mature while experiencing profound internal confusion about their true identity.

The *therapeutic challenge* lies in helping individuals recognize these patterns as symptoms rather than personality strengths. Many people with quiet BPD pride themselves on their independence, emotional control, and ability to function despite adversity. Learning to see these traits as potentially problematic defenses against emotional intimacy and authentic self-expression requires careful therapeutic exploration.

Clinical work with quiet BPD often begins with helping individuals recognize the cost of their high-functioning presentation. While their ability to maintain external stability has clear benefits, the internal price—chronic emotional pain, exhaustion, and disconnection from authentic self—typically proves unsustainable over time. The goal becomes finding ways to maintain functional capacity while developing more authentic emotional expression and self-connection.

Essential Points for Moving Forward

Quiet BPD represents a significant population of individuals whose internal struggles remain largely invisible to mental health systems designed to identify and treat more obvious presentations. The same emotional intensity, identity confusion, and interpersonal sensitivity that characterize classic BPD exist in these presentations but manifest through internalizing mechanisms that protect external functioning while creating severe internal distress.

Recognition of quiet BPD requires understanding that high functioning and emotional stability are not incompatible with significant psychological suffering. The ability to maintain employment, relationships, and social obligations while experiencing intense internal chaos reflects sophisticated coping mechanisms rather than the absence of psychological symptoms.

Treatment approaches must account for the unique challenges of working with individuals who have learned to hide their distress so effectively that they may not fully recognize it themselves. Standard assessment tools and crisis-focused interventions may miss this population entirely, requiring more nuanced approaches to identification and treatment planning.

The next step involves learning to recognize the subtle signs that suggest quiet BPD in loved ones—patterns that may have been dismissed as personality traits or stress responses but actually represent significant internal struggles that benefit from understanding and appropriate support.

Chapter 2: Recognizing Quiet BPD in Your Loved One

Clinical assessment of quiet borderline presentations requires attention to subtle behavioral patterns and internal experiences that often masquerade as personality strengths or minor stress responses. Research demonstrates that family members frequently notice changes in their loved one's behavior months or years before clinical symptoms become apparent to outside observers (Gunderson et al., 2018). These early recognition patterns typically involve shifts in perfectionism, emotional availability, and interpersonal engagement that can appear positive or neutral rather than concerning.

The challenge for families lies in distinguishing between normal stress responses, other mental health conditions, and the specific constellation of symptoms that characterize quiet BPD. Unlike classic borderline presentations that involve obvious emotional dysregulation and interpersonal conflict, quiet BPD symptoms often present as admirable traits taken to problematic extremes. The family member who suddenly becomes obsessively organized, extremely helpful, or emotionally distant may be developing sophisticated defense mechanisms against underlying borderline symptoms rather than simply maturing or adapting to life stress.

Signs Others Miss: Internalized Symptoms vs External Behaviors

Traditional borderline personality disorder identification relies heavily on external behavioral markers that disrupt social functioning or create obvious distress. Quiet BPD operates through *internalized symptom expression* that maintains social functioning while creating significant internal suffering (Fossati et al., 2014). Family members must learn to recognize these internalized presentations because they often represent the only observable indicators of underlying emotional turmoil.

Emotional regulation differences provide the clearest distinction between quiet and classic BPD presentations. Rather than explosive emotional outbursts, individuals with quiet BPD demonstrate what appears to be exceptional emotional control. They may rarely show anger, sadness, or frustration, even in situations where these responses would be appropriate and healthy. This emotional flatness often gets interpreted as maturity or strength, but closer observation reveals an artificial quality to their emotional responses.

Perfectionist behaviors serve as external markers of internal emotional chaos. The individual with quiet BPD may become obsessively focused on work performance, home organization, or physical appearance as a way to maintain control over their internal emotional state. This perfectionism often appears suddenly or intensifies significantly during periods of increased stress or interpersonal difficulty. Family members may notice that minor imperfections trigger disproportionate internal distress, even if the individual doesn't express this distress outwardly.

Social withdrawal patterns in quiet BPD differ from depression or social anxiety. Rather than avoiding social situations entirely, these individuals may engage socially but in a controlled, performative manner. They attend family gatherings, work events, and social activities but seem emotionally absent or overly focused on appearing perfect. Family members often describe feeling like they're interacting with a polished version of their loved one rather than the authentic person they once knew.

Self-sacrifice behaviors become exaggerated in quiet BPD presentations. The individual may become the family caretaker, always available to help others while never expressing their own needs. This helping behavior often has a compulsive quality—they seem unable to say no to requests for assistance, even when these requests interfere with their own well-being. This pattern typically intensifies during periods when their internal emotional state becomes more unstable.

Communication changes provide subtle but important indicators of quiet BPD development. These individuals may become excessively agreeable, rarely expressing opinions that might create conflict or disagreement. They often develop a habit of asking what others want or need while avoiding questions about their own preferences. Family conversations may feel one-sided, with the individual focusing entirely on others' experiences while revealing little about their own internal state.

Sleep and eating patterns frequently change in ways that suggest emotional dysregulation masked as health consciousness or productivity. The individual may develop rigid sleep schedules, extreme dietary restrictions, or exercise compulsions that appear to be healthy lifestyle choices but actually serve as emotional regulation mechanisms. Family members may notice that disruptions to these routines trigger significant anxiety or internal distress.

The Perfectionist Facade and Fear of Abandonment

Perfectionism in quiet BPD serves multiple psychological functions, primarily as a defense against the core fear of abandonment that characterizes all borderline presentations. Clinical observations reveal that these individuals develop the belief that perfect performance will prevent others from leaving or criticizing them (Sherry et al., 2013). This perfectionism extends beyond simple high standards to encompass an all-or-nothing approach to performance that creates constant internal pressure and frequent feelings of failure.

Performance-based self-worth becomes the foundation of identity in quiet BPD presentations. These individuals measure their value entirely through external achievements and others' approval. A single criticism or perceived disappointment from others can trigger intense shame and self-attack that may last for days or weeks. Family members often notice that their loved one seems unable to accept compliments genuinely but dwells extensively on any negative feedback.

Emotional caretaking represents a sophisticated form of abandonment prevention. The individual with quiet BPD becomes exquisitely attuned to others' emotional states and needs, often anticipating problems before they occur and working to solve them preemptively. This emotional caretaking extends to managing others' feelings about them—they may work constantly to ensure that everyone around them feels happy, comfortable, and satisfied with their presence.

Conflict avoidance strategies in quiet BPD can appear as exceptional interpersonal skills but actually represent fear-based behaviors designed to prevent any situation that might lead to relationship loss. These individuals may agree with others even when they disagree internally, avoid expressing needs that might inconvenience others, and go to extreme lengths to prevent any interpersonal friction. Family members may notice that their loved one has difficulty engaging in healthy disagreement or negotiation.

Identity shifting occurs as a response to perceived expectations from different people in their lives. The individual with quiet BPD may present differently to family members, coworkers, friends, and romantic partners, adapting their personality to match what they believe each person wants from them. This chameleon-like quality can make it difficult for family members to identify their loved one's authentic preferences, values, or personality traits.

Hypervigilance to social cues manifests as an almost supernatural ability to read others' moods and intentions. While this sensitivity can appear as exceptional empathy or social intelligence, it actually reflects constant monitoring for signs of disapproval, boredom, or withdrawal. The individual may notice facial expressions, tone changes, or body language shifts that others miss entirely, then spend hours analyzing what these cues might mean about the relationship.

Preemptive rejection behaviors occur when the individual with quiet BPD senses potential abandonment. Rather than fighting for the relationship or expressing their fears directly, they may begin withdrawing emotionally or creating distance as a way to protect themselves from anticipated rejection. Family members may notice periods where their loved one becomes less available or emotionally present without any obvious trigger.

Self-Assessment Tools for Families

Recognizing quiet BPD in a loved one requires systematic observation of behavioral patterns over time rather than single incidents or obvious crisis situations. Family members need tools to assess subtle changes and patterns that may indicate underlying emotional dysregulation masked by high-functioning behaviors (Zanarini, 2009). These assessment approaches must account for the internalized nature of symptoms while avoiding assumptions about the individual's internal experience.

Behavioral observation checklists help families track patterns that may indicate quiet BPD:

Emotional Expression Patterns:

- Does your loved one rarely show negative emotions, even in situations where such feelings would be appropriate?

- Do they seem to have difficulty expressing anger, sadness, or frustration directly?

- Have their emotional responses become more controlled or artificial over time?

- Do they appear emotionally flat or disconnected during conversations about feelings?

Perfectionist Behaviors:

- Has your loved one become increasingly focused on flawless performance in work, home, or personal areas?

- Do they seem unable to tolerate mistakes or imperfections in themselves?

- Have they developed rigid routines or standards that cause distress when disrupted?

- Do they spend excessive time on tasks to ensure perfect completion?

Interpersonal Patterns:

- Does your loved one seem to always prioritize others' needs over their own?

- Have they become increasingly agreeable, rarely expressing differing opinions?

- Do they appear to change their personality or preferences based on who they're with?

- Are they excessively concerned with how others perceive them?

Communication assessment involves evaluating how the individual expresses needs, preferences, and emotions:

Direct Expression:

- Can your loved one state their needs clearly and directly?

- Do they express preferences about activities, food, entertainment, or other choices?

- Are they able to disagree with others without excessive anxiety or avoidance?

- Can they discuss their emotions and internal experiences openly?

Indirect Communication:

- Do they often ask what others want without stating their own preferences?

- Are their communications primarily focused on others' experiences and needs?

- Do they use self-deprecating humor or minimize their own importance frequently?

- Are they more likely to hint at problems rather than addressing them directly?

Stress response evaluation examines how the individual handles challenges and pressure:

Internal Processing:

- Do they appear to handle stress well externally but show signs of internal struggle?

- Are there physical symptoms (headaches, fatigue, stomach problems) that increase during stressful periods?

- Do they withdraw emotionally during difficult times while maintaining their responsibilities?

- Are they more irritable or sensitive in private settings compared to public ones?

Coping Mechanisms:

- Have they developed rigid routines or control behaviors during stressful periods?

- Do they use perfectionism or overwork as ways to manage difficult emotions?

- Are they more likely to help others excessively when feeling distressed themselves?

- Do they engage in subtle self-punishment or self-denial during difficult times?

Differentiating from Anxiety, Depression, and Autism/ADHD

Quiet BPD shares symptom overlap with several other mental health conditions, creating diagnostic challenges for both family members and mental health professionals. Accurate recognition requires understanding the distinct patterns that characterize borderline presentations versus other conditions with similar surface manifestations (Paris, 2020). The key lies in examining the underlying motivations for behaviors and the specific constellation of symptoms rather than isolated traits.

Anxiety disorder differentiation focuses on the source and nature of worry patterns:

BPD-Related Anxiety:

- Primarily focused on relationship security and others' perceptions
- Intense fear of abandonment or rejection that drives behavioral choices
- Anxiety that increases in interpersonal situations or when alone
- Worry that centers on identity and self-worth rather than specific threats

Generalized Anxiety:

- Worry about multiple life areas including health, safety, and future events
- Anxiety that persists regardless of interpersonal context
- Physical symptoms that occur independently of relationship concerns
- Worry that focuses on specific, identifiable threats or scenarios

Depression comparison examines the nature of low mood and its triggers:

Quiet BPD Depression:

- Mood closely tied to interpersonal experiences and perceived rejection

- Ability to function normally in some contexts while struggling internally

- Depression that shifts based on relationship security and external validation

- Self-criticism and shame that focus on identity and worthiness rather than general hopelessness

Major Depression:

- Persistent low mood that affects multiple life areas consistently

- Difficulty functioning across most contexts during depressive episodes

- Hopelessness and sadness that persist regardless of external circumstances

- Cognitive symptoms like concentration problems and decision-making difficulties

Autism spectrum differentiation requires examining social difficulties and sensory sensitivities:

BPD Social Challenges:

- Hyperawareness of social cues with intense reactions to perceived rejection

- Social skills that appear normal or exceptional but require enormous energy to maintain

- Difficulty with authentic emotional expression rather than understanding social rules

- Social anxiety focused on abandonment rather than confusion about social expectations

Autism Spectrum Social Challenges:

- Difficulty reading social cues or understanding unwritten social rules

- Consistent social communication differences across all contexts

- Preference for routine and predictability that isn't related to emotional regulation

- Sensory sensitivities that affect daily functioning independently of interpersonal concerns

ADHD distinction involves examining attention and impulse control patterns:

Quiet BPD Attention Issues:

- Difficulty concentrating during emotional distress or interpersonal conflict

- Hyperfocus on perfectionist tasks or others' emotional needs

- Attention problems that fluctuate based on emotional state and relationship security

- Impulse control issues primarily in emotional or interpersonal contexts

ADHD Attention Issues:

- Consistent attention difficulties across multiple contexts and situations

- Difficulty with sustained attention regardless of emotional state

- Impulsivity that affects multiple life areas, not just emotional expression

- Attention problems that improve with structure and external supports

Recognition Patterns and Family Responses

Family recognition of quiet BPD typically follows predictable patterns that reflect the subtle nature of symptoms and the individual's skill at maintaining external functioning. Clinical experience suggests that family members often sense something has changed in their loved one months or years before they can articulate specific concerns (Gunderson, 2009). This intuitive recognition usually begins with feeling that interactions have become different in ways that are difficult to define.

Early recognition phases typically involve family members noticing that their loved one seems "not quite themselves" without being able to identify specific problems. They may feel that conversations have become more superficial, that their loved one seems to be performing rather than genuinely engaging, or that emotional connections feel more distant despite the absence of obvious conflict.

Validation of family concerns requires taking these subtle observations seriously rather than dismissing them as minor personality changes or stress responses. Family members often possess the most detailed knowledge of their loved one's baseline personality and behavioral patterns, making their observations particularly valuable for early recognition of quiet BPD development.

Responsive approaches involve creating safe spaces for emotional expression without pressuring the individual to reveal more than they're comfortable sharing. This might include reducing criticism or judgment, increasing positive interactions, and demonstrating through actions that the relationship remains secure despite any emotional struggles.

The recognition process requires patience and consistent observation rather than direct confrontation about suspected symptoms. Quiet BPD often involves significant shame about internal experiences, making direct questioning about emotional states counterproductive. Instead, family members can focus on maintaining supportive relationships while remaining alert to opportunities for their loved one to share their internal experiences voluntarily.

Recognizing quiet BPD in a loved one represents the first step toward providing appropriate support and encouraging professional help when needed. The internalized nature of symptoms means that family observation often provides the primary avenue for identification, making family education about these presentations crucial for early recognition and intervention.

The goal of recognition is not diagnosis—that requires professional assessment—but rather developing an understanding that can inform more supportive responses and encourage appropriate professional consultation when indicated. Family members who understand quiet BPD presentations can provide more effective emotional support while avoiding responses that inadvertently reinforce perfectionist or people-pleasing behaviors.

Understanding the fear-based nature of many quiet BPD behaviors helps family members respond with compassion rather than frustration when their loved one seems distant, perfectionistic, or unable to express authentic emotions. This understanding forms the foundation for the next essential component: comprehending the neurobiological and developmental factors that create these presentations.

Chapter 3: The Science Behind Quiet BPD

Neurobiological research reveals that quiet borderline personality disorder involves the same fundamental brain differences as classic BPD presentations, but with distinct patterns of neural activation that promote internalizing rather than externalizing responses to emotional triggers (Schulze et al., 2016). Advanced neuroimaging studies demonstrate that individuals with quiet BPD show heightened activity in brain regions associated with self-criticism and emotional suppression, while classic BPD presentations show greater activation in areas linked to external emotional expression and behavioral impulses.

The development of quiet versus classic BPD presentations appears to depend on complex interactions between genetic vulnerability, early attachment experiences, and environmental factors that either encourage or discourage emotional expression (Crowell et al., 2009). Research indicates that individuals who develop quiet presentations often experienced early environments that rewarded emotional control and punished emotional expression, leading to sophisticated neural adaptations that favor internalization over externalization of distress.

Neurobiological Foundations Made Accessible

The brain differences underlying quiet BPD involve complex interactions between emotional processing centers and regulatory systems that most people never need to understand in detail. However, grasping basic patterns helps families comprehend why their loved one might struggle with issues that seem simple on the surface, and why certain approaches to support prove more effective than others.

The emotional brain versus the thinking brain provides a useful framework for understanding BPD neurobiology. All humans have an emotional processing system centered in the limbic area that responds quickly to threats and opportunities, and a regulatory system in the prefrontal cortex that provides reasoning, planning, and emotional control. In quiet BPD, these systems show specific patterns of interaction that create the characteristic internalized symptoms (Hazlett et al., 2012).

Amygdala hyperactivity occurs in all BPD presentations, including quiet variants. The amygdala serves as the brain's alarm system, scanning for threats and triggering emotional responses. In BPD, this system operates at heightened sensitivity, perceiving danger in situations that others might experience as neutral or mildly stressful. A coworker's distracted greeting might trigger the same neural alarm response as a genuine threat, flooding the system with stress hormones and intense emotions.

Prefrontal cortex adaptations differ between quiet and classic BPD presentations. While classic BPD often involves decreased prefrontal activity during emotional episodes, quiet BPD typically shows *overactive* prefrontal regulation. This means the thinking brain works overtime to control and suppress emotional responses generated by the hyperactive alarm system. This overcontrol creates the appearance of emotional stability while the individual experiences intense internal struggle.

Default mode network differences help explain the constant internal analysis characteristic of quiet BPD. The default mode network activates when the brain isn't focused on external tasks, typically involved in self-reflection and internal processing. In quiet BPD, this network shows altered patterns that support constant self-monitoring and rumination about relationships and personal performance (Carpenter & Trull, 2013).

Neurotransmitter systems involved in mood regulation also show distinct patterns in quiet BPD. Serotonin, which affects mood stability and impulse control, often functions differently than in classic presentations. Rather than contributing to impulsive behaviors, serotonin dysregulation in quiet BPD tends to support obsessive thinking patterns and emotional suppression. This creates the internal chaos while maintaining behavioral control that characterizes these presentations.

Stress hormone patterns reflect the constant internal activation that occurs in quiet BPD. Cortisol, the primary stress hormone, often remains chronically elevated due to persistent emotional monitoring and suppression. This chronic activation explains the physical exhaustion that many individuals with quiet BPD experience despite appearing to handle stress well externally.

How Trauma Creates Internalized Patterns

Trauma's impact on brain development creates the neurobiological foundation for quiet BPD presentations, but the specific patterns of internalization versus externalization depend on the type, timing, and context of traumatic experiences. Research demonstrates that quiet BPD often develops from what clinicians term *complex developmental trauma*—chronic relational injuries that occur during critical periods of brain development rather than single traumatic events (van der Kolk, 2014).

Early relational trauma shapes neural development in ways that promote emotional suppression and hypervigilance to others' emotional states. Children who experience inconsistent caregiving, emotional neglect, or criticism for emotional expression develop brain patterns that prioritize others' emotional needs over their own internal experiences. The developing nervous system adapts by creating sophisticated monitoring systems for external threats while suppressing internal emotional awareness.

Emotional invalidation during childhood creates specific neural adaptations that characterize quiet BPD presentations. When caregivers consistently dismiss, minimize, or punish a child's emotional expressions, the developing brain learns that emotions are dangerous and must be controlled or hidden. This leads to overdevelopment of emotional suppression systems and underdevelopment of healthy emotional expression pathways (Linehan, 2014).

Attachment disruption affects the brain's capacity for emotional regulation and interpersonal connection. Secure attachment provides the foundation for healthy emotional development, teaching children that emotions are manageable and that relationships remain stable despite emotional expression. Disrupted attachment creates neural patterns of hypervigilance and emotional suppression designed to maintain connection with unpredictable or emotionally unavailable caregivers.

Perfectionism as trauma response develops when children learn that perfect performance provides the only reliable way to maintain caregiver approval and avoid criticism or abandonment. The brain adapts by creating neural pathways that support obsessive attention to performance while suppressing authentic emotional needs and expressions that might threaten these crucial relationships.

Hypervigilance systems develop as adaptive responses to environments where emotional safety depends on constant monitoring of others' emotional states and needs. Children learn to read subtle cues about caregivers' moods and adjust their behavior accordingly, developing neural patterns that support this external focus while neglecting internal emotional awareness and expression.

Identity formation disruption occurs when children must suppress authentic aspects of themselves to maintain crucial relationships. The brain regions involved in self-recognition and identity development become oriented toward external validation rather than internal awareness, creating the identity confusion and external focus characteristic of quiet BPD presentations.

The Role of Attachment in Quiet BPD Development

Attachment theory provides a framework for understanding how early relational experiences shape the specific neural and behavioral patterns that characterize quiet BPD presentations. Research indicates that individuals with quiet BPD often experienced attachment relationships that provided basic safety and security but lacked emotional attunement and validation of internal experiences (Fonagy et al., 2016).

Dismissive attachment patterns frequently precede quiet BPD development. Children with caregivers who provide physical care and stability but struggle with emotional intimacy learn to suppress their emotional needs and focus on maintaining approval through performance and compliance. These children develop neural patterns that support emotional independence while maintaining hypervigilance to relationship security.

Parentification experiences create specific attachment disruptions that promote quiet BPD presentations. Children who become emotional caretakers for their parents or family systems develop sophisticated skills for reading and managing others' emotions while learning to suppress their own needs. This role reversal creates neural adaptations that support external focus and emotional suppression.

Conditional love patterns teach children that approval and security depend on meeting specific expectations or maintaining particular presentations. The developing brain adapts by creating systems that constantly monitor performance and external approval while suppressing authentic aspects of self that might threaten these conditional relationships. This creates the perfectionist presentations common in quiet BPD.

Emotional overwhelm in caregivers can lead to attachment patterns that promote emotional suppression in children. When caregivers struggle with their own emotional regulation, children may learn that their emotional expressions add burden to an already overwhelmed system. This teaches the developing brain to prioritize others' emotional capacity over their own emotional needs.

Avoidant strategies develop as adaptive responses to attachment relationships that provide security only when emotional needs remain hidden or minimized. Children learn that emotional expression

25

threatens relationship stability, leading to neural patterns that support emotional suppression and external focus while maintaining connection through performance and compliance.

Mentalization deficits result from attachment relationships that lack reflection on internal experiences. Mentalization—the ability to understand mental states underlying behavior—develops through relationships where caregivers help children understand and articulate their internal experiences. Without this development, individuals struggle to recognize and express their own emotions while becoming hyperattuned to others' emotional states.

Evidence-Based Understanding Without Clinical Jargon

The scientific foundation of quiet BPD helps explain why certain family responses prove more helpful than others and why recovery requires specific types of therapeutic intervention. Understanding these patterns allows families to provide more effective support while avoiding responses that inadvertently reinforce problematic neural patterns.

Brain plasticity research demonstrates that the neural patterns underlying quiet BPD can change throughout life with appropriate interventions and relational experiences. The brain's capacity for adaptation means that individuals with quiet BPD can develop healthier emotional regulation and expression patterns, though this process requires time, patience, and often professional support.

Therapeutic neuroplasticity occurs when individuals engage in activities that promote new neural pathway development. Dialectical behavior therapy (DBT), specifically designed for borderline presentations, creates measurable changes in brain function that support improved emotional regulation and interpersonal effectiveness (Goodman et al., 2014). These changes typically require consistent practice over months or years.

Relational healing involves providing the attuned, consistent emotional responses that were missing during critical developmental periods. Family members can contribute to this healing by maintaining emotional availability, validating internal experiences, and responding to emotional expressions with acceptance rather than judgment or advice.

Stress reduction interventions prove particularly important for quiet BPD because chronic stress hormone activation interferes with neural healing and adaptation. Regular exercise, adequate sleep, mindfulness practices, and reduced interpersonal conflict all support the brain changes necessary for recovery from quiet BPD presentations.

Environmental modifications can support neural healing by reducing triggers for the hypervigilance and emotional suppression systems that characterize quiet BPD. This might involve creating predictable routines, reducing criticism and conflict, and increasing positive interactions that don't require emotional performance from the individual.

Recovery timeline expectations need to account for the time required for significant neural change. While individuals with quiet BPD can experience symptom improvement relatively quickly with appropriate support, fundamental changes in emotional regulation and expression patterns typically require months to years of consistent intervention and practice.

The scientific understanding of quiet BPD provides hope by demonstrating that these presentations result from adaptive responses to difficult circumstances rather than permanent personality flaws. The same neural plasticity that allowed the brain to adapt to challenging early environments can support healing and healthier functioning when provided with appropriate therapeutic and relational experiences.

Translating Science into Family Support

Understanding the neurobiological foundations of quiet BPD helps families develop more effective and compassionate responses to their loved one's struggles. The scientific evidence demonstrates that symptoms reflect sophisticated adaptations to challenging circumstances rather than personal weaknesses or character flaws, allowing family members to respond with understanding rather than frustration or judgment.

Validation of internal experiences becomes crucial when understood in the context of developmental trauma and attachment disruption. Family members can support healing by acknowledging and accepting their loved one's internal experiences without trying to fix or change them immediately. This validation helps reverse the early learning that emotions are dangerous or unacceptable.

Patient response expectations reflect understanding that neural change requires time and consistent practice. Family members who understand the biological basis of quiet BPD can maintain supportive responses even when progress seems slow or inconsistent. Recovery from these presentations typically involves gradual changes rather than sudden improvements.

Environmental stability supports the neural healing process by reducing stress hormone activation and allowing the brain's adaptive systems to function more effectively. Families can contribute by maintaining predictable routines, reducing conflict, and creating safe spaces for emotional expression without pressure or judgment.

The scientific foundation provides a roadmap for understanding how quiet BPD develops and what types of interventions support recovery. This knowledge forms the basis for developing effective family responses and understanding how professional treatment approaches target the specific neural and behavioral patterns that characterize these presentations.

Moving Forward with Scientific Understanding

The neurobiological research on quiet BPD demonstrates that these presentations involve real, measurable brain differences that explain the apparent contradictions between external functioning and internal distress. This scientific foundation validates both the individual's struggle and the family's observations while providing hope through evidence of the brain's capacity for healing and change.

Understanding the attachment and trauma foundations of quiet BPD helps families recognize that their loved one's symptoms represent adaptive responses to challenging circumstances rather than character defects or personal choices. This understanding forms the foundation for developing more effective family responses that support healing rather than inadvertently reinforcing problematic patterns.

The next step involves applying this scientific understanding to practical family strategies that support recovery while maintaining healthy relationships. Understanding how quiet BPD affects family systems and interpersonal relationships provides the foundation for developing specific approaches that benefit both the individual and their loved ones.

Chapter 4: How Quiet BPD Affects Relationships

Research on borderline personality disorder relationships reveals that quiet presentations create unique interpersonal challenges distinct from classic BPD dynamics. Studies indicate that partners and family members of individuals with quiet BPD report higher levels of confusion and uncertainty compared to those involved with classic presentations, primarily because the emotional intensity remains hidden while interpersonal effects persist (Hooley & Gotlib, 2000). Unlike relationships characterized by obvious conflict and dramatic episodes, quiet BPD relationships often appear stable on the surface while involving significant underlying tension and emotional disconnection.

Clinical observations demonstrate that quiet BPD affects relationships through *subtle erosion patterns* rather than explosive conflicts. Family members frequently describe feeling like they're "walking on eggshells" despite the absence of obvious triggers or dramatic responses. This creates a unique form of relational stress where loved ones sense problems but cannot identify specific behaviors or incidents that explain their discomfort (Gunderson & Lyons-Ruth, 2008).

The Emotional Rollercoaster for Loved Ones

Living with someone who has quiet BPD creates a distinctive emotional experience for family members that differs significantly from other mental health conditions. The apparent stability and high functioning of the individual with quiet BPD creates cognitive dissonance for loved ones who sense underlying distress but cannot reconcile this intuition with external presentations.

Invisible tension characterizes much of the family experience with quiet BPD. Loved ones often report feeling like something is "off" or "different" about their relationship without being able to identify specific problems. This creates a sense of unease that persists despite the absence of obvious conflict or dysfunction. Family members may question their own perceptions, wondering if they're being overly sensitive or imagining problems that don't exist.

Emotional responsibility burden frequently develops as family members unconsciously take on the role of maintaining their loved one's emotional stability. Without realizing it, they may begin monitoring their own behavior to avoid triggering hidden emotional responses in the individual with quiet BPD. This creates exhaustion and resentment that family members often struggle to understand since their loved one appears emotionally stable and rarely makes direct demands.

Intermittent reinforcement patterns occur when the individual with quiet BPD occasionally reveals their internal emotional state, providing brief glimpses of their true experience before returning to their controlled presentation. These moments of authenticity can be both relieving and concerning for family members, who may feel gratified to finally see the "real" person while simultaneously worried about the intensity of emotions revealed.

Performance pressure affects family relationships when the individual with quiet BPD's perfectionism extends to family functioning. Family members may feel pressure to maintain a certain image or level of performance to avoid triggering their loved one's internal distress. This can manifest as pressure to keep the house perfect, avoid conflict, or present a happy family image to others.

Emotional invalidation concerns arise when family members struggle to respond appropriately to their loved one's needs because those needs remain largely unexpressed. The individual with quiet BPD may expect their family to intuitively understand their

31

emotional state and provide support without direct communication. When family members fail to meet these unexpressed needs, both parties may feel frustrated and misunderstood.

Anticipatory anxiety develops in family members who learn to constantly monitor for subtle signs of their loved one's emotional state. This hypervigilance creates ongoing stress as family members attempt to prevent problems they cannot clearly identify or predict. The energy required for this constant monitoring can be exhausting and ultimately unsustainable.

Walking on Eggshells with Someone Who Seems Fine

The phenomenon of walking on eggshells typically involves obvious triggers and dramatic responses that teach family members which behaviors to avoid. With quiet BPD, this dynamic becomes more complex because the "eggshells" are invisible and the responses are internalized rather than externalized. This creates a confusing situation where family members sense they need to be careful but cannot identify what they're being careful about.

Subtle trigger identification becomes a primary challenge for family members trying to maintain family harmony. Unlike classic BPD where triggers often involve obvious themes like abandonment or criticism, quiet BPD triggers may be extremely subtle—a slightly different tone of voice, a delayed response to a text message, or even positive attention given to another family member. These triggers can seem arbitrary or unpredictable to family members.

Internal response recognition requires family members to become expert observers of minimal behavioral changes that might indicate their loved one is experiencing internal distress. This might involve noticing slight changes in posture, facial expressions, or energy levels that suggest emotional upset despite the absence of obvious emotional expression. The subtle nature of these cues makes accurate reading extremely difficult.

Behavioral adaptation patterns develop as family members unconsciously modify their behavior to minimize their loved one's internal distress. This might involve avoiding certain topics of conversation, maintaining specific routines, or carefully managing their own emotional expressions to prevent triggering their loved one's abandonment fears or perfectionist anxiety.

Communication hypervigilance occurs when family members begin carefully monitoring their own words, tone, and timing to avoid inadvertently causing internal distress in their loved one. This creates artificial communication patterns where spontaneous expression becomes difficult, and every interaction requires careful consideration of potential impact.

Confusion about boundaries arises because the individual with quiet BPD rarely expresses their limits or needs directly. Family members may unknowingly cross boundaries they didn't know existed, leading to internal distress in their loved one that manifests as withdrawal, increased perfectionism, or subtle emotional unavailability rather than direct communication about the boundary violation.

Emotional labor intensification occurs as family members take on increasing responsibility for maintaining family emotional stability without clear guidance about how to do so effectively. This invisible emotional work can become overwhelming, particularly when family members receive little acknowledgment or appreciation for their efforts since their loved one may not recognize the extent of their own impact on family dynamics.

Common Relationship Patterns and Cycles

Quiet BPD relationships tend to follow predictable patterns that can persist for months or years without obvious crisis points or resolution. These cycles often involve gradual emotional distance followed by attempts at reconnection, but without the dramatic ruptures and repairs characteristic of classic BPD presentations (Zanarini et al., 2007).

The distance-pursue cycle represents one of the most common patterns in quiet BPD relationships. The individual with quiet BPD may gradually withdraw emotionally when they perceive threats to the relationship or feel overwhelmed by internal emotions. This withdrawal often appears as increased work focus, social commitments, or emotional unavailability rather than obvious rejection. Family members typically respond by pursuing connection, which may inadvertently increase the individual's sense of pressure and lead to further withdrawal.

Perfectionism-disappointment spirals occur when the individual with quiet BPD sets impossibly high standards for themselves or their relationships, then experiences internal devastation when these standards aren't met. Family members may not even realize standards existed until they notice their loved one becoming distant or self-critical. These cycles can persist without resolution because the standards often remain unspoken and therefore cannot be addressed directly.

Caretaking-resentment patterns develop when family members unconsciously take on emotional caretaking responsibilities to maintain their loved one's stability. The individual with quiet BPD may become dependent on this caretaking while simultaneously resenting the dependence. Family members often feel trapped between continuing to provide support they know isn't healthy and risking their loved one's emotional destabilization by setting boundaries.

Performance-authenticity conflicts arise when the individual with quiet BPD maintains their high-functioning facade within the family while family members sense the artificiality of this presentation. Family members may feel like they're living with a performer rather than an authentic person, leading to intimacy difficulties and relationship dissatisfaction that can be difficult to address without appearing to criticize their loved one's coping mechanisms.

Crisis-avoidance cycles occur when both the individual with quiet BPD and their family members become focused on preventing any situation that might trigger emotional overwhelm. This can lead to increasingly restricted family functioning as more topics, activities, or situations become off-limits to maintain emotional stability. While this prevents obvious crises, it also prevents authentic relationship development and problem-solving.

Validation-seeking behaviors may emerge as the individual with quiet BPD indirectly attempts to confirm their worth and relationship security without directly asking for reassurance. This might involve excessive helping, perfect performance in family roles, or subtle fishing for compliments. Family members often sense these needs but may struggle to provide appropriate responses that don't reinforce problematic patterns.

Case Studies from Real Families

Clinical experience reveals consistent patterns in how quiet BPD affects different types of family relationships. These patterns provide insight into the specific challenges faced by various family members and the adaptations that develop over time to manage these complex dynamics.

Spousal relationship case study: A married couple in their forties sought counseling for what they described as growing emotional distance despite the absence of obvious conflict. The spouse with quiet BPD maintained perfect household management, career success, and social presentation while gradually becoming less emotionally available to their partner. The partner reported feeling like they were living with a roommate rather than a spouse, despite their loved one's consistent kindness and reliability.

The partner described walking on eggshells without understanding why, carefully monitoring their own behavior to maintain harmony they couldn't clearly define. They reported feeling exhausted by constant emotional vigilance despite their spouse's apparent stability. The relationship had developed a pattern where the partner increasingly handled emotional labor while the spouse focused on external performance, creating growing resentment and disconnection.

Parent-child relationship dynamics: A parent with quiet BPD maintained excellent external functioning while struggling with internal emotional regulation that affected their parenting in subtle ways. The adult child reported feeling like they had to be "perfect" to maintain their parent's approval, despite the parent never directly expressing criticism or disapproval. The child had learned to suppress their own needs and emotions to protect their parent from perceived stress.

The adult child described feeling responsible for their parent's emotional well-being without understanding why or how this responsibility had developed. They reported difficulty setting boundaries or expressing disagreement because they sensed these actions caused their parent internal distress, even though the parent never directly expressed this distress or asked them to modify their behavior.

Sibling relationship patterns: Adult siblings of an individual with quiet BPD often develop complementary roles within the family system. One sibling described becoming the family "problem solver" while their sibling with quiet BPD became the "successful one." This division allowed each sibling to occupy a distinct niche but created pressure for both to maintain their roles rigidly.

The sibling without BPD reported feeling overshadowed by their loved one's apparent success while simultaneously worried about their well-being. They described sensing that their sibling's achievements came at a significant emotional cost but feeling unable to address this concern directly. Family gatherings became exercises in maintaining surface-level harmony while avoiding topics that might trigger their sibling's internal distress.

Workplace relationship impacts: Colleagues of individuals with quiet BPD often describe them as ideal coworkers who are reliable, helpful, and professionally competent. However, closer working relationships may reveal the subtle signs of internal struggle. A supervisor described noticing that their employee with quiet BPD seemed to take minor feedback as devastating criticism, despite maintaining professional demeanor and excellent work quality.

Coworkers reported feeling like they needed to be especially careful with their communication style around this individual, though they couldn't explain why. Team dynamics often shifted to accommodate the individual's apparent sensitivity without direct communication about needs or boundaries. This created workplace relationships that functioned well on the surface but lacked authentic collaboration and open communication.

Family System Adaptations

Families living with quiet BPD typically develop sophisticated adaptation patterns that maintain stability while accommodating the unique challenges these presentations create. These adaptations often become so automatic that family members don't recognize them as responses to mental health symptoms rather than normal family functioning.

Role specialization frequently occurs as family members unconsciously take on specific functions that support the individual with quiet BPD's emotional regulation. One family member might become the emotional barometer, monitoring and reporting on family emotional climate. Another might serve as the buffer, handling potentially stressful situations before they reach their loved one. These roles often develop organically without explicit discussion or recognition.

Communication modification happens gradually as family members learn to adjust their communication style to minimize their loved one's internal distress. This might involve avoiding certain topics, using specific tones or approaches, or timing conversations carefully. While these modifications often improve family harmony, they can also restrict authentic communication and prevent important issues from being addressed.

Conflict avoidance systems develop as families learn that even minor disagreements can cause significant internal distress for their loved one with quiet BPD. Families may establish unspoken rules about avoiding criticism, disagreement, or challenging conversations. While this maintains surface harmony, it can prevent healthy problem-solving and relationship growth.

Emotional labor distribution often becomes imbalanced as other family members take on increasing responsibility for maintaining family emotional stability. This might involve managing their own emotions more carefully, providing extra emotional support to other family members, or taking on tasks that their loved one finds emotionally challenging. This redistribution can create resentment and exhaustion over time.

Building Healthier Dynamics

Understanding the specific ways quiet BPD affects family relationships provides the foundation for developing more effective responses that support both the individual and their loved ones. The goal isn't to eliminate all challenges but rather to create more sustainable and authentic relationship patterns that acknowledge the reality of quiet BPD while maintaining healthy boundaries and communication.

Recognition of patterns represents the first step toward building healthier family dynamics. When family members understand that their intuitive sense of "walking on eggshells" reflects real interpersonal dynamics rather than their own oversensitivity, they can begin to address these patterns more effectively. This recognition validates their experience while providing direction for positive change.

Authentic communication development involves gradually increasing direct expression of needs, feelings, and boundaries while maintaining sensitivity to their loved one's internal experience. This requires patience and skill as family members learn to balance honesty with compassion, avoiding both emotional suppression and overwhelming confrontation.

Boundary establishment becomes crucial for maintaining family member well-being while supporting their loved one's recovery. This involves recognizing the difference between helpful support and enabling behaviors, setting limits on emotional caretaking responsibilities, and maintaining their own emotional health and authentic expression.

The next step involves understanding the specific challenges family members face as caregivers and developing strategies for maintaining their own well-being while providing appropriate support. Recognizing when helping becomes enabling and learning effective self-care approaches forms the foundation for sustainable family relationships with quiet BPD.

Chapter 5: The Caregiver's Dilemma

Family caregiving research demonstrates that loved ones of individuals with quiet BPD face unique challenges that differ significantly from other caregiving situations. Studies indicate that caregivers of people with internalized mental health presentations report higher levels of uncertainty, emotional exhaustion, and role confusion compared to caregivers dealing with more obvious symptoms (Pearlin et al., 1990). The absence of clear behavioral indicators of distress makes it difficult for family members to know when help is needed, what type of support would be most beneficial, and when their efforts might actually be counterproductive.

Clinical observations reveal that well-intentioned family members often inadvertently reinforce problematic patterns in quiet BPD by providing support that reduces external consequences of emotional suppression while failing to address underlying issues. This creates a caregiving paradox where the most natural and compassionate responses may actually perpetuate the symptoms they're intended to help (Hooley & Hoffman, 1999).

When Helping Becomes Enabling

The distinction between helpful support and enabling behaviors becomes particularly complex with quiet BPD because the individual's high functioning can mask their dependence on others' emotional labor. Unlike situations where enabling involves obvious behaviors like covering for substance use or violent outbursts, quiet BPD enabling often involves subtle emotional support that maintains the individual's ability to suppress authentic emotions while avoiding the natural consequences of this suppression.

Emotional labor absorption represents one of the most common forms of enabling in quiet BPD relationships. Family members may unconsciously take on responsibility for maintaining emotional stability that the individual with quiet BPD cannot or will not manage themselves. This might involve constantly monitoring the emotional climate, managing other family members' reactions, or providing excessive reassurance about relationship security and personal worth.

Consequence prevention occurs when family members shield their loved one from natural results of their emotional suppression and perfectionist behaviors. This might involve taking over responsibilities when perfectionism creates paralysis, managing social situations to prevent their loved one from experiencing criticism, or handling conflict resolution because their loved one cannot tolerate disagreement. While these interventions prevent immediate distress, they also prevent the individual from developing healthy coping mechanisms.

Performance support systems develop when families organize around maintaining their loved one's high-functioning facade rather than encouraging authentic emotional expression. This might involve helping maintain perfect household standards, managing schedules to prevent overwhelm, or avoiding topics or situations that might challenge their loved one's emotional control. These supports can become enabling when they prevent the individual from learning to function with less than perfect emotional regulation.

Crisis avoidance behaviors become enabling when family members work harder than their loved one to prevent emotional overwhelm or interpersonal conflict. This might involve walking on eggshells to avoid triggering abandonment fears, managing other relationships to prevent their loved one from experiencing rejection, or avoiding necessary conversations because they might cause emotional distress.

Validation without boundaries occurs when family members provide constant reassurance about their loved one's worth, competence, or relationship security without encouraging the development of internal validation skills. While validation is important, excessive external validation can prevent individuals with quiet BPD from developing the ability to tolerate uncertainty or self-soothe during periods of emotional distress.

Responsibility displacement happens when family members take on tasks or decisions that their loved one could manage themselves but chooses to avoid due to perfectionist anxiety or fear of making mistakes. This might involve handling financial decisions, managing social commitments, or making choices about household matters. While this support reduces immediate stress, it can reinforce their loved one's belief that they cannot handle normal life responsibilities.

Managing Your Own Mental Health

Caring for someone with quiet BPD creates specific mental health challenges for family members that require recognition and active management. The subtle nature of symptoms and the high-functioning presentation can make it difficult for caregivers to justify their own need for support, leading to isolation and burnout that develops gradually over months or years.

Caregiver stress identification requires recognizing symptoms that may not seem obviously connected to their loved one's mental health condition. Caregivers may experience chronic fatigue, difficulty making decisions, social withdrawal, or physical symptoms like headaches and digestive problems without recognizing these as stress responses. The absence of obvious crises or dramatic symptoms in their loved one can make it difficult to identify the source of their own distress.

Emotional boundary confusion frequently affects family members who struggle to distinguish between their own emotions and their loved one's internal experience. The hypervigilance required to monitor subtle emotional cues can lead to emotional enmeshment where caregivers lose touch with their own feelings and needs. This creates anxiety, depression, and identity confusion that may require professional support to resolve.

Validation of caregiver experience becomes essential because others may not understand the stress involved in caring for someone who appears to function well. Friends and extended family may not recognize the emotional labor required or may dismiss concerns about someone who seems successful and stable. This lack of external validation can lead caregivers to question their own perceptions and minimize their legitimate need for support.

Stress response recognition involves learning to identify physical and emotional symptoms that indicate caregiver burnout before it becomes severe. This might include changes in sleep patterns, increased irritability, difficulty concentrating, or loss of interest in previously enjoyed activities. Early recognition allows for intervention before stress becomes overwhelming or affects other relationships.

Professional support utilization may be necessary for caregivers dealing with the unique challenges of quiet BPD. This might involve individual therapy to process their experiences, support groups for family members of people with mental health conditions, or consultation with mental health professionals about effective caregiving strategies. The invisible nature of quiet BPD symptoms makes professional guidance particularly valuable.

Relationship maintenance with other family members and friends becomes important for preventing the social isolation that can develop when caregiving demands consume increasing amounts of time and emotional energy. Maintaining these relationships provides emotional support, perspective, and practical assistance that can prevent caregiver burnout and provide relief from constant vigilance.

Setting Boundaries with Someone Who Internalizes Everything

Boundary setting with quiet BPD presents unique challenges because traditional boundary violations may not occur, while subtle emotional intrusions can be difficult to identify and address. The individual with quiet BPD may not directly ask for inappropriate support or make obvious demands, but their emotional suppression may create pressure for family members to provide constant emotional regulation support.

Emotional boundaries require particular attention because the individual with quiet BPD may unconsciously expect family members to manage emotions they cannot or will not express directly. This might involve expecting others to intuitively know their emotional state, provide reassurance without being asked, or modify their behavior to prevent causing internal distress. Setting boundaries around emotional responsibility requires clear communication about what family members can and cannot provide.

Communication boundaries become necessary when the individual with quiet BPD communicates primarily through behavior rather than direct expression. Family members may need to establish limits on their availability for emotional problem-solving, require direct communication about needs rather than expecting others to guess, or refuse to engage in conversations that are primarily focused on managing the individual's anxiety or perfectionist concerns.

Support boundaries involve distinguishing between reasonable requests for help and expectations that family members will maintain their loved one's emotional stability. This might mean refusing to take on responsibilities that the individual could manage themselves, setting limits on the amount of reassurance provided, or requiring that their loved one develop their own coping strategies before providing support.

Time and energy boundaries protect caregivers from the exhaustion that can develop from constant emotional monitoring and support provision. This might involve scheduling specific times for emotional conversations rather than being available constantly, taking breaks from caregiving responsibilities, or engaging in activities that restore rather than drain emotional energy.

Consequence boundaries allow natural results of emotional suppression and perfectionist behaviors to occur rather than protecting their loved one from these outcomes. This might involve allowing them to experience the stress of perfectionist standards rather than helping maintain these standards, refusing to solve problems that result from their avoidance behaviors, or allowing them to manage their own emotional reactions to normal life stressors.

Boundary communication strategies must account for the individual's tendency to internalize criticism and their fear of abandonment. Boundaries need to be presented as expressions of love and concern rather than rejection, with clear explanations of how these limits will benefit the relationship long-term. The focus should be on maintaining healthy connection rather than creating distance or punishment.

Self-Care Strategies That Actually Work

Effective self-care for caregivers of individuals with quiet BPD must address the specific stresses created by this situation while being realistic about the ongoing nature of these challenges. Traditional self-care approaches may not adequately address the hypervigilance, emotional exhaustion, and role confusion that characterize this caregiving experience.

Energy management requires recognition that emotional monitoring and regulation support require significant mental and physical energy that must be replenished regularly. This might involve scheduling periods of reduced emotional availability, engaging in activities that restore rather than drain energy, and creating physical spaces where constant vigilance is not required. Energy management also involves recognizing early signs of depletion and taking action before exhaustion becomes overwhelming.

Emotional processing support helps caregivers manage the complex feelings that arise from loving someone whose internal experience differs dramatically from their external presentation. This might involve therapy, support groups, journaling, or trusted relationships where caregivers can express frustration, confusion, and concern without judgment. Regular emotional processing prevents the buildup of resentment and burnout that can damage relationships.

Perspective maintenance involves regular connection with people and activities outside the caregiving role to maintain a sense of identity and normalcy. This might include maintaining friendships, pursuing hobbies, or engaging in work or volunteer activities that provide a sense of competence and satisfaction. Perspective maintenance helps prevent the tunnel vision that can develop when caregiving becomes the primary focus of life.

Stress reduction techniques specifically designed for the hypervigilance that characterizes this type of caregiving include mindfulness practices that focus on present-moment awareness rather than constant monitoring of others' emotional states. This might involve meditation, progressive muscle relaxation, or breathing exercises that help caregivers disengage from constant emotional surveillance.

Physical health protection becomes essential because the stress of caring for someone with quiet BPD can manifest in physical symptoms that develop gradually over time. This involves maintaining regular exercise, adequate sleep, proper nutrition, and medical care that addresses stress-related symptoms before they become serious health problems. Physical health provides the foundation for sustained emotional caregiving.

Professional consultation can provide caregivers with strategies specific to their situation and validation of their experiences. This might involve individual therapy, family therapy, or consultation with mental health professionals who understand borderline presentations. Professional support can help caregivers distinguish between helpful and enabling behaviors while developing more effective approaches to their loved one's needs.

Creating Sustainable Caregiving Patterns

Long-term caregiving success requires developing patterns that can be maintained over months and years without causing caregiver burnout or relationship deterioration. This involves finding the balance between providing appropriate support and maintaining healthy boundaries that protect both the caregiver and the individual with quiet BPD.

Role clarity involves establishing clear expectations about what caregivers will and will not provide, both for themselves and their loved one. This might include defining specific types of support that are appropriate, establishing time limits on emotional availability, or requiring reciprocal consideration of caregiver needs. Role clarity prevents the mission creep that can gradually expand caregiving responsibilities beyond sustainable limits.

Support system development extends beyond the immediate family to include friends, extended family, professional resources, and community connections that can provide assistance, perspective, and relief. This might involve educating other family members about quiet BPD so they can provide appropriate support, connecting with support groups for families affected by mental health conditions, or developing relationships with mental health professionals who can provide guidance.

Communication skill development helps caregivers learn more effective ways to interact with their loved one that promote healthy independence while maintaining emotional connection. This might involve learning validation techniques that don't reinforce dependence, developing assertiveness skills for setting boundaries, or practicing ways to express concern without taking responsibility for their loved one's emotional state.

Expectation management involves accepting the long-term nature of quiet BPD while maintaining hope for improvement and recovery. Caregivers need realistic expectations about the pace of change, the ongoing nature of support needs, and their own limitations in providing help. This prevents the disappointment and burnout that can result from expecting rapid or dramatic improvements.

Crisis planning helps families prepare for periods when their loved one's emotional suppression becomes unsustainable and internal distress increases significantly. This might involve identifying early warning signs of increased instability, establishing plans for professional intervention, or developing strategies for maintaining family functioning during difficult periods. Crisis planning reduces anxiety and provides structure during chaotic times.

The goal of sustainable caregiving is to provide appropriate support while maintaining the caregiver's own well-being and encouraging their loved one's healthy independence. This requires ongoing attention to the balance between support and enablement, regular assessment of caregiver needs, and willingness to adjust strategies as situations change over time.

Moving Toward Effective Communication

Understanding the caregiver's dilemma provides the foundation for developing more effective communication strategies that support the individual with quiet BPD while protecting caregiver well-being. The next step involves learning specific communication techniques that validate internalized emotions while encouraging healthy expression and authentic connection.

Effective communication with quiet BPD requires understanding how to speak in ways that penetrate emotional suppression without triggering defensive responses. This involves learning the specific language patterns, validation techniques, and conversation approaches that promote openness while respecting the individual's need for emotional control.

Chapter 6: Communication That Connects

Research on communication patterns in families affected by borderline personality disorder reveals that traditional therapeutic communication techniques often prove insufficient for quiet presentations, where emotional suppression and perfectionist facades create barriers to authentic expression (Rnic et al., 2018). Studies demonstrate that standard validation and active listening approaches may actually reinforce emotional suppression in quiet BPD by allowing individuals to maintain their controlled presentation while receiving emotional support that doesn't challenge their defensive patterns.

Effective communication with quiet BPD requires understanding the unique defensive structures that maintain emotional suppression while creating subtle pathways for authentic expression that don't trigger abandonment fears or perfectionist anxiety. Clinical observations indicate that successful communication approaches must validate internal experiences without reinforcing the belief that emotions are dangerous while creating safety for gradual emotional expression (Linehan, 2014).

Speaking the Language of Quiet BPD

Communication with individuals who have quiet BPD requires understanding the specific ways they process information and the defensive filters that shape their interpretation of others' words and intentions. Their hypervigilance to criticism, abandonment cues, and perceived expectations creates a communication environment where subtle word choices and nonverbal cues carry disproportionate weight.

Indirect expression recognition becomes essential because individuals with quiet BPD rarely state their needs, feelings, or concerns directly. Instead, they communicate through behavior, subtle cues, and indirect statements that require careful attention to decode. A comment about being "fine" may actually indicate significant distress, while excessive helping behavior might signal fear of abandonment or feelings of inadequacy.

Emotional translation skills help family members understand the underlying emotions behind controlled presentations. When someone with quiet BPD appears calm and competent while clearly struggling internally, family members need to recognize the disconnect between presentation and experience. This might involve noticing subtle signs of stress, fatigue, or anxiety that the individual isn't expressing verbally.

Safety-first communication acknowledges that individuals with quiet BPD often suppress emotions because expression feels dangerous to their relationships or self-image. Communication approaches must create sufficient safety for emotional expression while respecting their need for control. This means avoiding pressure for immediate emotional disclosure while creating opportunities for gradual sharing when they feel ready.

Perfectionism-sensitive language avoids words and phrases that might trigger the individual's perfectionist anxiety or fear of criticism. This includes avoiding absolute terms like "always" or "never," being careful about tone and timing, and framing observations as concerns rather than criticisms. The goal is to communicate clearly while minimizing triggers for emotional suppression.

Validation of internal experience requires acknowledging the reality of their internal struggle even when external presentation suggests otherwise. This might involve statements like "I can see this is important to you" or "It seems like you're putting a lot of energy into this" that validate their effort and internal experience without requiring them to admit struggling or express emotions directly.

Response patience allows for the delayed emotional processing that characterizes quiet BPD. Individuals may need time to process communications internally before responding authentically. Rushing for immediate responses or interpretations can trigger defensive suppression and controlled presentations that prevent authentic connection.

Validation Techniques for Internalized Emotions

Traditional validation approaches focus on reflecting and acknowledging expressed emotions, but quiet BPD requires validation techniques that address unexpressed internal experiences without pressuring for emotional disclosure. This creates a unique communication challenge where family members must validate what they sense rather than what they directly observe.

Behavioral validation acknowledges the effort and energy required to maintain high functioning despite internal struggles. This might involve recognizing their hard work, appreciating their reliability, or acknowledging the strength required to manage their responsibilities. This type of validation supports their positive behaviors while implicitly recognizing the internal cost of maintaining these standards.

Effort recognition validates the emotional labor involved in maintaining emotional control and high functioning. Statements like "You put so much care into everything you do" or "I can see how much this matters to you" acknowledge their internal investment without requiring them to admit struggle or express vulnerability directly.

Strength-based validation focuses on acknowledging their coping abilities and resilience while gently opening space for emotional expression. This might involve statements like "You handle so much with such grace" followed by "and it's okay if you don't feel graceful all the time." This approach validates their current functioning while giving permission for imperfection.

Internal experience validation addresses the gap between external presentation and internal reality without requiring admission of struggle. Phrases like "That sounds really important to you" or "I can imagine that takes a lot of mental energy" validate their internal experience while respecting their need to maintain composure.

Emotional permission giving creates space for emotional expression without requiring it. This might involve statements like "It's okay to have mixed feelings about this" or "It would make sense if this felt overwhelming sometimes." This approach normalizes emotional responses while giving permission for authentic expression when they feel ready.

Timing validation acknowledges that emotional processing may happen differently for them than for others. Statements like "Take all the time you need to think about this" or "There's no rush to figure this out right now" validate their processing style while removing pressure for immediate emotional responses.

What NOT to Say and What to Say Instead

Communication with quiet BPD requires avoiding common phrases and approaches that trigger defensive responses while learning alternative expressions that create safety and openness. Many well-intentioned communication attempts can inadvertently reinforce emotional suppression or trigger abandonment fears.

Avoid pressure phrases that demand immediate emotional expression or disclosure:

Instead of: "How are you really feeling?" (implies their stated feelings aren't real) Say: "I'm here if you want to talk about anything" (offers availability without pressure)

Instead of: "You seem upset" (forces acknowledgment of emotions they may not be ready to express) Say: "I'm wondering how this is sitting with you" (gentle inquiry without assumption)

Instead of: "You don't have to be perfect" (may feel invalidating of their coping strategy) Say: "Your effort means a lot to me" (validates their approach while implying acceptance of imperfection)

Avoid minimizing statements that dismiss their internal experience:

Instead of: "You're overthinking this" (invalidates their processing style) Say: "You really think things through carefully" (validates their thoroughness)

Instead of: "Just relax" (implies their stress is a choice) Say: "This seems really important to you" (validates their internal experience)

Instead of: "It's not that serious" (dismisses their internal reaction) Say: "I can see this matters to you" (acknowledges their perspective)

Avoid criticism disguised as concern:

Instead of: "You're too hard on yourself" (may feel like criticism of their coping style) Say: "You care so much about doing things well" (validates their motivation)

Instead of: "You need to express your feelings more" (creates pressure and implies inadequacy) Say: "I appreciate when you share your thoughts with me" (reinforces positive communication without pressure)

Avoid assumptions about their experience:

Instead of: "I know you're struggling" (assumes knowledge of their internal state) Say: "I care about how you're doing" (expresses concern without assumption)

Instead of: "You must be exhausted" (assumes their experience) Say: "You've been handling a lot lately" (acknowledges their situation without assumption)

Replacement communication strategies focus on creating safety and validation:

Use curiosity instead of assumption: "I'm curious about your perspective on this" Offer support without pressure: "I'm here if you need anything" Validate effort over outcomes: "I can see how much thought you put into this" Express appreciation for sharing: "Thank you for telling me about this" Normalize complexity: "This sounds like a complex situation"

Scripts for Difficult Conversations

Quiet BPD creates specific challenges for addressing problems, expressing concerns, or having conversations that might trigger emotional responses. These scripts provide frameworks for approaching difficult topics while minimizing triggers for emotional suppression or abandonment fears.

Expressing concern about their well-being:

Opening: "I've been thinking about you lately and wanted to check in. I know you handle things really well, and I'm here if you ever want to talk about anything that's on your mind."

Follow-up if they deflect: "I appreciate how capable you are, and I also care about how you're doing underneath all that capability. There's no pressure to talk about anything specific - I just want you to know I'm here."

Closing: "Take your time thinking about it. I'm not going anywhere, and there's no pressure to share anything you're not ready to share."

Addressing perfectionist patterns:

Opening: "I've noticed how much care and effort you put into everything you do. Your attention to detail is really impressive. I'm wondering if sometimes all that effort feels heavy?"

If they minimize: "I'm not suggesting you should care less - your standards are part of what makes you who you are. I'm just thinking about whether there are ways to make it feel a little easier sometimes."

Supporting statement: "Whatever you decide, I want you to know that my appreciation for you isn't based on everything being perfect. I value you as a person, not just for what you accomplish."

Setting boundaries while maintaining connection:

Opening: "I want to talk about something because our relationship is important to me, and I want to make sure we're both taking care of ourselves in it."

Boundary statement: "I've realized that I've been [specific behavior], and I think it might not be the most helpful way for me to support you. I'm thinking it might be better if I [alternative approach]."

Reassurance: "This isn't about caring less or backing away from you. It's about finding ways to support you that work better for both of us long-term."

Addressing emotional suppression patterns:

Opening: "I've been thinking about how strong you are and how well you handle difficult situations. I admire that about you, and I also want you to know that it's okay with me if you don't always feel strong."

Permission giving: "I want you to know that our relationship can handle whatever you're really feeling. You don't have to protect me from your emotions or present in any particular way for me to care about you."

Support offer: "I'm here for whatever version of you shows up - the capable version, the uncertain version, the frustrated version, or any other version. They're all welcome with me."

Addressing enabling patterns:

Opening: "I've been thinking about how I can best support you, and I wonder if I've been doing some things that might not actually be helpful in the long run."

Explanation: "I care about you, and because I care, I want to make sure I'm supporting your strength and capability rather than accidentally taking over things you can handle yourself."

Collaborative approach: "I'm wondering if we could talk about what kind of support actually feels helpful to you versus what might feel like I don't trust you to handle things."

Communication Timing and Environment

The success of difficult conversations with quiet BPD often depends as much on timing and environment as on the specific words used. These individuals require sufficient emotional safety and predictability to engage authentically while managing their fear of abandonment and need for control.

Optimal timing considerations include periods when the individual appears relatively stable and isn't dealing with external stressors that might overwhelm their emotional regulation capacity. Avoid initiating difficult conversations during times of obvious stress, major life changes, or when they're already dealing with perfectionist anxiety about specific situations.

Environmental safety factors include private settings where they won't feel observed or judged by others, familiar environments where they feel comfortable, and times when there won't be interruptions or time pressure. The physical environment should support emotional safety while providing easy exit options if they become overwhelmed.

Preparation strategies help ensure conversations are as productive as possible. This includes thinking through the main points beforehand, considering their likely concerns or reactions, and preparing responses that maintain connection while addressing necessary topics. Preparation also involves managing your own emotional state to remain calm and supportive throughout the conversation.

Follow-up approaches recognize that individuals with quiet BPD may need time to process conversations internally before responding authentically. This might involve checking in after a few days without pressure for specific responses, acknowledging any sharing they do provide, and maintaining consistent availability without pursuing immediate resolution.

Building Long-Term Communication Patterns

Effective communication with quiet BPD requires consistency over time rather than perfect individual conversations. The goal is building trust and safety that gradually allows for more authentic expression while respecting their need for emotional control and their fear of abandonment.

Trust building happens through consistent, patient responses that validate their experience without pressuring for change. This includes following through on commitments, maintaining emotional availability without being intrusive, and responding to any emotional sharing with appreciation rather than advice or attempts to fix their problems.

Emotional safety development occurs as they learn that authentic expression doesn't lead to criticism, abandonment, or demands for immediate change. This requires family members to manage their own reactions to emotional disclosures while providing consistent acceptance and support for whatever the individual chooses to share.

Pattern recognition helps family members notice what communication approaches work best for their specific loved one while remaining flexible as needs change over time. This includes paying attention to their responses to different communication styles, timing, and topics while adjusting approaches based on feedback and outcomes.

The ultimate goal of effective communication is creating relationship dynamics that support gradual healing and authentic connection while respecting the individual's current coping strategies and their need for emotional safety. This foundation of improved communication creates the possibility for addressing more complex relationship patterns and supporting recovery over time.

Moving Forward with Connection

Effective communication provides the foundation for all other interventions and support strategies in quiet BPD relationships. When family members learn to speak in ways that create safety rather than triggering defensive responses, they create possibilities for addressing underlying issues while maintaining healthy relationship dynamics.

The next step involves applying these communication principles to specific therapeutic approaches and practical strategies that support recovery while maintaining family well-being. Understanding how evidence-based treatments work and how families can support these interventions creates a comprehensive approach to quiet BPD that benefits everyone involved.

Chapter 7: DBT Skills for Families

Research on dialectical behavior therapy (DBT) demonstrates that while the intervention was specifically designed for individuals with borderline personality disorder, the core skills prove equally valuable for family members navigating these complex relationships. Studies indicate that when family members learn and practice DBT skills, both individual and family functioning improve significantly compared to families where only the identified patient receives treatment (Hoffman et al., 2005). The four modules of DBT—mindfulness, distress tolerance, emotion regulation, and interpersonal effectiveness—provide practical frameworks that address the specific challenges families face when living with quiet BPD presentations.

Clinical observations reveal that family members often develop their own emotional dysregulation patterns in response to living with someone who has internalized BPD symptoms. The hypervigilance, emotional suppression, and interpersonal walking-on-eggshells that characterize these family dynamics create stress responses that benefit from the same skill-building approaches used in formal BPD treatment (Fruzzetti & Fruzzetti, 2003).

Adapting Dialectical Behavior Therapy for Loved Ones

DBT skills require modification when applied to family members because their goals differ from those of individuals in treatment for BPD. While the person with quiet BPD works on emotional regulation and authentic expression, family members need skills for maintaining their own emotional stability while providing appropriate support without enabling problematic patterns.

Mindfulness adaptations for families focus on developing awareness of their own emotional responses and triggers rather than becoming expert observers of their loved one's internal state. Family mindfulness practice involves noticing when they're operating from anxiety, guilt, or the compulsive need to fix or manage their loved one's emotional experience. This awareness creates space for choosing responses rather than reacting automatically to perceived emotional distress.

Present-moment awareness for family members involves staying grounded in current reality rather than anticipating future emotional crises or rehashing past relationship difficulties. This includes practicing the ability to engage with their loved one as they are in the moment rather than through the filter of diagnostic understanding or family history. Present-moment awareness prevents the anticipatory anxiety that can dominate family interactions.

Dialectical thinking application helps family members hold multiple truths simultaneously—their loved one is both struggling and capable, both in need of support and responsible for their own emotional regulation, both deserving of compassion and accountable for their impact on family relationships. This balanced perspective prevents the extreme thinking that can lead to either overwhelming caretaking or emotional withdrawal.

Radical acceptance practice for families involves accepting the reality of their loved one's condition while maintaining hope for improvement. This includes accepting their own limitations in providing help, the pace of recovery, and the ongoing nature of BPD symptoms. Radical acceptance doesn't mean passive resignation but rather clear-eyed engagement with actual circumstances rather than wished-for realities.

Non-judgmental stance development helps family members observe their loved one's behaviors and their own responses without automatically categorizing them as good or bad, healthy or unhealthy. This perspective reduces the emotional reactivity that can escalate family conflicts while maintaining the ability to set appropriate boundaries and provide effective support.

Effectiveness focus teaches family members to evaluate their responses based on whether they achieve desired outcomes rather than whether they feel morally right or emotionally satisfying. This might involve choosing not to provide reassurance when it reinforces anxiety, setting boundaries even when it causes short-term distress, or refusing to engage in emotional caretaking that prevents their loved one from developing independent coping skills.

Distress Tolerance When Your Person is in Crisis

Family members living with quiet BPD need specific distress tolerance skills because crises often manifest internally rather than through obvious external behaviors. Traditional crisis management approaches may not apply when the individual maintains external functioning while experiencing severe internal distress that affects the entire family system.

Crisis recognition skills help family members identify when their loved one is experiencing internal emotional overwhelm despite maintained external presentation. This includes noticing subtle changes in behavior, energy, communication patterns, or physical presentation that suggest internal distress. Early recognition allows for appropriate support without waiting for obvious crisis indicators that may never appear in quiet presentations.

TIPP skills adaptation (Temperature, Intense exercise, Paced breathing, Paired muscle relaxation) provides families with immediate tools for managing their own emotional responses when sensing their loved one's internal crisis. These physiological interventions help family members avoid reactive responses that might escalate the situation or reinforce problematic patterns while maintaining their capacity for thoughtful support.

Distraction techniques for families focus on temporarily shifting attention away from their loved one's emotional state when direct intervention isn't helpful or appropriate. This might involve engaging in activities that provide emotional relief, connecting with friends outside the family system, or focusing on tasks that create a sense of competence and control. Distraction prevents the rumination and hypervigilance that can exhaust family members.

Self-soothing practices help family members manage the anxiety, guilt, and helplessness that often arise when their loved one is struggling internally. This includes developing personal comfort rituals, creating physical environments that promote emotional regulation, and practicing activities that restore emotional equilibrium. Self-soothing prevents family members from seeking emotional regulation through managing their loved one's experience.

Improve the moment strategies provide ways to find meaning and hope during difficult periods when family functioning feels strained or when their loved one's recovery seems stalled. This might involve focusing on small improvements, connecting with personal values about family relationships, or finding ways to contribute positively to family functioning despite ongoing challenges.

Pros and cons analysis helps family members make decisions about when to intervene, when to step back, and how to balance their own needs with their desire to support their loved one. This rational approach prevents impulsive decisions made from anxiety or guilt while ensuring that family responses align with long-term relationship goals rather than immediate emotional relief.

Emotion Regulation for the Whole Family

Living with quiet BPD often creates emotional dysregulation throughout the family system as members unconsciously mirror their loved one's internal emotional intensity or develop reactive patterns in response to the subtle interpersonal dynamics. Family emotion regulation skills focus on maintaining individual emotional health while supporting healthy family functioning.

Emotional awareness development helps family members distinguish between their own emotions and those they sense in their loved one. This includes learning to identify emotional responses that belong specifically to them versus reactions to their loved one's internal state. Clear emotional boundaries prevent the emotional enmeshment that can develop when family members unconsciously absorb their loved one's unexpressed emotions.

Emotion labeling practice involves developing vocabulary and awareness for the complex emotional experiences that arise in families affected by quiet BPD. This includes identifying emotions like anticipatory anxiety, compassion fatigue, grief for relationship losses, frustration with invisible symptoms, and guilt about setting boundaries. Accurate labeling enables more effective emotional regulation strategies.

Opposite action implementation helps family members respond effectively when their emotional impulses conflict with their long-term relationship goals. This might involve approaching their loved one when instinct says to withdraw, setting boundaries when guilt demands accommodation, or expressing needs when anxiety suggests self-suppression. Opposite action breaks destructive emotional cycles that can maintain problematic family patterns.

Pleasant activities scheduling becomes essential for family members who may unconsciously restrict their own enjoyment to match their loved one's internal struggle or to remain available for emotional support. Regular engagement in personally meaningful activities prevents the emotional depletion that can make family members unable to provide sustainable support.

Emotional regulation in relationships focuses on managing emotional responses during family interactions without suppressing authentic feelings or taking responsibility for others' emotional reactions. This includes learning to express concern without anxiety, set boundaries without guilt, and maintain emotional connection without enmeshment.

Vulnerability reduction strategies help family members identify and address factors that increase their susceptibility to emotional overwhelm or reactive patterns. This might involve managing stress in other life areas, maintaining physical health, addressing unresolved grief about family changes, or developing support systems outside the immediate family.

Interpersonal Effectiveness with Quiet BPD Dynamics

Standard interpersonal effectiveness skills require adaptation for the unique dynamics created by quiet BPD, where traditional assertiveness approaches may trigger abandonment fears or emotional suppression while indirect communication styles can reinforce problematic patterns.

DEAR MAN modifications (Describe, Express, Assert, Reinforce, Mindful, Appear confident, Negotiate) need adjustment for quiet BPD interactions where direct assertion might trigger emotional shutdown while indirect approaches may enable continued emotional suppression. The key lies in finding approaches that communicate clearly while maintaining emotional safety for all family members.

Describing observations with quiet BPD requires focusing on specific behaviors and their impact rather than interpretations of internal emotional states. This might involve statements like "I've noticed you've been working longer hours lately" rather than "You seem stressed." This approach validates observable reality without forcing acknowledgment of internal experiences the individual may not be ready to discuss.

Expressing feelings in families affected by quiet BPD involves sharing your own emotional experience without demanding emotional reciprocity or immediate response. This models emotional expression while respecting their need for processing time. The goal is authentic communication rather than emotional extraction or fixing.

Asserting needs requires particular sensitivity because direct requests may trigger perfectionist anxiety or fear of disappointing others. Effective assertion with quiet BPD often involves offering choices, providing context for requests, and expressing confidence in their ability to meet reasonable needs while accepting their decision-making autonomy.

Reinforcement strategies focus on acknowledging positive interactions and authentic emotional expressions when they occur, rather than trying to create motivation for change. This might involve expressing appreciation when they share feelings, acknowledging their efforts to communicate, or validating their perspectives when they offer them voluntarily.

GIVE skills (Gentle, Interested, Validate, Easy manner) prove particularly important in quiet BPD family dynamics where interpersonal sensitivity runs high and abandonment fears operate beneath the surface. These approaches maintain relationship connection while addressing necessary topics and expressing authentic family member needs.

Relationship maintenance during difficult conversations requires balancing honesty with reassurance, addressing problems while affirming relationship security, and expressing concerns while validating their efforts and capabilities. The goal is problem-solving that strengthens rather than threatens family connections.

Family DBT Practice Implementation

Successful DBT skill implementation requires regular practice and adaptation to specific family dynamics rather than expecting immediate mastery or perfect application. The goal is gradual development of more effective response patterns that support both individual and family well-being over time.

Daily mindfulness practice can become a family activity that models emotional regulation without targeting anyone's specific symptoms. This might involve brief meditation periods, mindful eating practices, or shared reflection time that demonstrates the value of present-moment awareness while creating positive family experiences.

Skill generalization involves applying DBT concepts to normal family situations rather than waiting for crisis situations. This includes using emotion regulation skills during everyday stressors, practicing interpersonal effectiveness during routine family decisions, and implementing distress tolerance during minor conflicts or disappointments.

Family skill coaching involves family members supporting each other's skill practice without becoming responsible for each other's emotional regulation. This might include gentle reminders about breathing techniques during stress, celebrating successful skill application, or providing encouragement when someone struggles with implementation.

Progress tracking focuses on family relationship improvements rather than individual symptom reduction. This includes noticing increased authentic communication, reduced family conflict, improved emotional connections, and enhanced problem-solving effectiveness. Progress measurement validates family efforts while maintaining focus on achievable goals.

Creating Sustainable Practice Patterns

Long-term success with family DBT skills requires developing sustainable practice patterns that can be maintained during both stable and challenging periods. The goal is integration into daily family life rather than crisis-only implementation that may be forgotten when most needed.

Routine integration involves building skill practice into existing family activities rather than creating additional obligations that may be abandoned during stressful periods. This might include incorporating mindfulness into shared meals, practicing distress tolerance during family entertainment, or using interpersonal effectiveness during household decision-making.

Flexibility maintenance allows for adaptation of skill practice based on changing family circumstances, individual energy levels, and varying stress situations. This prevents perfectionist approaches to skill implementation that can create additional family pressure while maintaining commitment to ongoing practice and improvement.

Family meeting structures provide regular opportunities for practicing interpersonal effectiveness skills while addressing family functioning issues. These meetings can focus on appreciation sharing, problem-solving, and coordination rather than attempting to address individual mental health symptoms directly.

Individual skill development remains important alongside family practice because each family member needs personal emotional regulation capabilities that don't depend on others' participation or cooperation. This includes individual mindfulness practice, personal distress tolerance resources, and individual approaches to interpersonal effectiveness.

Professional Integration and Support

Family DBT skill practice works best when coordinated with professional treatment rather than replacing it. Understanding how to support professional interventions while maintaining appropriate boundaries helps families contribute to recovery without overstepping their role.

Therapist coordination involves understanding how family skill practice can complement professional treatment without interfering with therapeutic relationships or treatment goals. This might include sharing observations about skill practice success, asking for guidance about family implementation, or requesting clarification about appropriate family support approaches.

Boundary maintenance with professional treatment helps families stay within their appropriate role while supporting their loved one's therapy participation. This includes avoiding attempts to be their loved one's therapist, respecting confidentiality boundaries, and focusing on family relationship improvements rather than symptom management.

Crisis plan coordination ensures that family DBT skills align with professional crisis intervention plans rather than conflicting with treatment recommendations. This involves understanding when to use family skills versus when to seek professional support, and how to implement distress tolerance while maintaining safety.

The integration of DBT skills into family life provides practical tools for managing the unique challenges created by quiet BPD while supporting both individual and family well-being. These skills create the foundation for the next step—developing environmental modifications that support recovery while maintaining healthy family functioning.

Chapter 8: Creating a Supportive Environment

Environmental psychology research demonstrates that physical and social environments significantly impact emotional regulation capacity, particularly for individuals with heightened emotional sensitivity such as those with quiet BPD. Studies indicate that environmental modifications can reduce stress hormone activation, improve emotional stability, and support therapeutic progress when designed to address specific neurobiological vulnerabilities (Ulrich et al., 2018). Unlike general stress reduction approaches, environments supporting quiet BPD recovery must balance sensory calm with opportunities for authentic emotional expression while avoiding reinforcement of isolation or emotional suppression patterns.

Clinical observations reveal that individuals with quiet BPD often create highly controlled environments that support their emotional suppression while inadvertently increasing their sensitivity to environmental changes or disruptions. Effective supportive environments maintain stability and predictability while gradually increasing tolerance for normal life unpredictability and emotional expression (Meaney-Tavares & Haseley, 2019).

Home Strategies That Reduce Internal Chaos

Home environment modifications for quiet BPD must address the internal emotional turbulence that remains invisible to outside observers while avoiding environmental controls that reinforce emotional avoidance or perfectionist patterns. The goal is creating spaces that support emotional regulation without enabling emotional suppression.

Sensory environment optimization focuses on reducing environmental stressors that can overwhelm already heightened emotional sensitivity. This includes managing lighting to avoid harsh fluorescents that can increase anxiety, controlling noise levels to prevent overstimulation, and creating spaces with comfortable textures and temperatures that support emotional comfort. These modifications reduce the sensory load that can push someone with quiet BPD toward emotional overwhelm.

Organization systems that support emotional regulation differ from perfectionist organization that creates anxiety when disrupted. Effective organization provides predictable structure that reduces decision fatigue and cognitive load while maintaining flexibility for normal life changes. This might involve creating designated spaces for important items, developing routines that support daily functioning, and establishing systems that can be maintained even during periods of emotional difficulty.

Emotional expression spaces provide areas where authentic feelings can be experienced and expressed safely without affecting other family members. This might include a private room for emotional processing, outdoor spaces for physical expression of emotions, or creative areas where feelings can be expressed through art, music, or writing. These spaces normalize emotional expression while respecting the individual's need for privacy and control.

Communication zones establish areas and times that support authentic family communication while respecting everyone's emotional needs. This might involve creating comfortable seating arrangements that facilitate conversation, establishing regular family meeting spaces, or designating certain areas as technology-free zones that encourage face-to-face interaction.

Safety and comfort elements address the hypervigilance and emotional sensitivity that characterize quiet BPD without creating environments so controlled that they increase sensitivity to normal life disruptions. This includes ensuring privacy for emotional processing, creating spaces that feel secure and protected, and establishing environmental predictability that supports emotional regulation without fostering rigidity.

Flexibility integration maintains the structure needed for emotional regulation while building tolerance for normal household changes and unpredictability. This involves creating core environmental supports that remain consistent while allowing for seasonal changes, family activities, and normal life variations that prevent environmental rigidity.

Workplace Accommodations and Advocacy

Professional environments present unique challenges for individuals with quiet BPD because their high functioning may mask their need for accommodations while workplace stressors can significantly impact their internal emotional regulation. Effective workplace strategies must support their professional success while addressing their emotional regulation needs.

Accommodation identification focuses on modifications that support emotional regulation without revealing personal information about mental health conditions. This might include requesting flexible scheduling to manage stress periods, obtaining permission for brief breaks during emotionally challenging situations, or securing workspace modifications that reduce sensory overload or interpersonal stress.

Communication strategies with supervisors and colleagues require balancing transparency with privacy while ensuring necessary support. This might involve discussing general stress management needs without disclosing specific mental health information, requesting accommodations framed in terms of productivity optimization, or working with human resources to identify available supports without full disclosure.

Performance management during emotional regulation difficulties requires strategies that maintain professional functioning while managing internal distress. This includes developing systems for managing perfectionist anxiety about work quality, creating backup plans for periods of increased emotional sensitivity, and establishing realistic expectations about performance consistency.

Interpersonal navigation in workplace settings addresses the social challenges created by quiet BPD's impact on relationships while maintaining professional boundaries. This might involve managing fear of criticism or rejection from supervisors, developing strategies for workplace conflict resolution, and maintaining appropriate emotional boundaries with colleagues.

Stress management integration involves implementing emotional regulation strategies that can be used discretely in professional settings. This includes developing brief mindfulness practices that can be used during work breaks, identifying environmental modifications that support emotional regulation, and creating systems for managing overwhelming situations without disrupting work responsibilities.

Legal protection understanding helps individuals understand their rights regarding workplace accommodations for mental health conditions while making informed decisions about disclosure levels. This includes understanding ADA protections, knowing how to request reasonable accommodations, and accessing resources for workplace discrimination or accommodation denial.

Building a Support Network That Gets It

Social support networks for quiet BPD require careful consideration because the individual's high functioning can make it difficult for others to understand their support needs, while their emotional sensitivity can make traditional support approaches overwhelming or counterproductive.

Education of support network involves helping friends and family understand quiet BPD presentations without violating privacy or creating excessive focus on mental health symptoms. This might include sharing general information about internalized emotional presentations, explaining the disconnect between external functioning and internal experience, and providing guidance about helpful versus potentially harmful support approaches.

Boundary setting with supporters establishes clear expectations about what types of support are helpful while preventing well-meaning individuals from providing support that enables emotional suppression or creates additional pressure. This includes communicating about emotional processing needs, expressing preferences about advice-giving versus listening, and establishing limits on crisis support availability.

Professional support integration coordinates therapeutic relationships with informal support networks to ensure consistency and prevent conflicting approaches. This might involve sharing general treatment goals with close family members, ensuring that support approaches align with therapeutic recommendations, and maintaining appropriate boundaries between professional and personal support relationships.

Peer support development focuses on connecting with others who understand similar experiences while avoiding relationships based solely on shared mental health challenges. This might include participating in support groups for borderline personality disorder, connecting with others who understand high-functioning mental health presentations, or finding communities that share values about emotional authenticity and personal growth.

Crisis support planning establishes clear protocols for how support network members can help during periods of increased emotional distress while maintaining appropriate boundaries and professional support prioritization. This includes identifying early warning signs that supporters can recognize, establishing communication protocols for crisis situations, and clarifying roles during difficult periods.

Long-term relationship maintenance addresses the challenges of maintaining supportive relationships when internal struggles remain largely invisible to others. This includes strategies for maintaining connection during emotional withdrawal periods, communicating appreciation for ongoing support, and managing relationship changes that may occur during recovery.

Crisis Planning for Internal Storms

Crisis planning for quiet BPD requires recognition that crises often remain internal and invisible to outside observers while potentially being just as dangerous as external behavioral crises. Traditional crisis planning approaches may miss the unique warning signs and intervention needs of internalized emotional overwhelm.

Early warning sign identification focuses on subtle changes in behavior, communication, or functioning that may indicate increasing internal emotional distress before it reaches crisis levels. This might include changes in sleep patterns, increased perfectionist behaviors, social withdrawal, changes in communication patterns, or subtle shifts in emotional availability.

Internal crisis recognition involves developing awareness of the subjective experience of emotional overwhelm that characterizes quiet BPD crises. This includes recognizing when emotional suppression becomes unsustainable, when internal self-criticism reaches dangerous levels, when dissociation increases significantly, or when passive suicidal ideation intensifies.

Support network activation establishes protocols for engaging professional and personal support during internal crises that may not be obvious to others. This includes determining when to contact mental health professionals, identifying trusted individuals who can provide appropriate support, and establishing communication methods for requesting help when direct communication feels impossible.

Safety planning adaptation addresses the specific safety concerns related to internalized emotional crises rather than focusing solely on external behavioral risks. This includes strategies for managing overwhelming internal experiences, maintaining basic functioning during emotional storms, and accessing appropriate help when internal distress becomes unmanageable.

Professional intervention protocols establish clear guidelines for when internal emotional distress requires professional intervention versus when it can be managed with personal and family support. This includes understanding warning signs that indicate need for immediate professional help, knowing how to access crisis mental health services, and maintaining relationships with mental health professionals who understand quiet BPD presentations.

Recovery planning focuses on strategies for returning to stable functioning after internal emotional crises while learning from the experience to prevent future crises or improve crisis management. This includes debriefing about crisis triggers and effective interventions, adjusting ongoing support strategies based on crisis experiences, and integrating lessons learned into daily emotional regulation practices.

Family System Environment Modifications

Creating supportive environments extends beyond individual accommodations to include modifications in family system functioning that support recovery while maintaining healthy relationships for all family members. These changes must balance the needs of the individual with quiet BPD against the needs of other family members.

Communication environment changes establish family communication patterns that support authentic emotional expression while maintaining emotional safety for all family members. This might involve establishing regular family meetings for open communication, creating guidelines for addressing conflict constructively, and developing family practices that normalize emotional expression and discussion.

Emotional regulation modeling involves family members demonstrating healthy emotional regulation strategies through their own behavior rather than focusing on teaching or correcting the individual with quiet BPD. This includes family members managing their own emotional responses effectively, demonstrating authentic emotional expression, and showing how to handle stress and conflict in healthy ways.

Routine and structure balance creates family routines that provide stability and predictability while maintaining flexibility for individual needs and changing circumstances. This includes establishing consistent family activities that provide connection, creating predictable daily routines that support everyone's emotional regulation, and maintaining flexibility for individual emotional needs.

Stress reduction strategies focus on reducing family system stress that can impact everyone's emotional regulation capacity. This might involve managing family schedules to prevent overcommitment, addressing family conflicts constructively, and ensuring that family responsibilities are distributed fairly among capable family members.

Individual space respect ensures that each family member has access to private space and time for individual emotional regulation and processing. This includes respecting closed doors and privacy requests, allowing family members to temporarily withdraw from family activities when needed, and creating physical spaces where individuals can manage their emotional needs privately.

Environmental Flexibility and Adaptation

Supportive environments must maintain flexibility to adapt to changing needs during different phases of recovery while avoiding environmental rigidity that can increase stress and reduce emotional regulation capacity. The goal is creating environments that grow and change with recovery progress.

Gradual challenge introduction involves slowly increasing environmental complexity and unpredictability as emotional regulation capacity improves. This might include gradually introducing changes to routines, increasing social activities as tolerance improves, and expanding environmental experiences as emotional regulation skills strengthen.

Seasonal and temporal adaptations acknowledge that emotional regulation needs may change based on stress levels, life circumstances, and recovery progress. This includes adjusting environmental supports during high-stress periods, modifying approaches during different seasons or life stages, and maintaining flexibility in environmental strategies based on changing needs.

Growth accommodation ensures that environmental modifications support increasing independence and emotional expression rather than reinforcing dependence or emotional suppression. This includes gradually reducing environmental controls as emotional regulation improves, encouraging increasing responsibility for environmental management, and supporting expansion of comfort zones and environmental tolerance.

The creation of supportive environments provides the foundation for successful professional treatment and family support strategies. Understanding how environmental modifications support recovery while avoiding reinforcement of problematic patterns helps families create contexts that promote healing and growth. The next step involves understanding how to access and advocate for professional treatment that recognizes and addresses quiet BPD presentations effectively.

Chapter 9: Professional Help That Understands Quiet BPD

Mental health research reveals significant gaps in professional recognition and treatment of quiet borderline personality disorder presentations, with studies indicating that these individuals often receive multiple incorrect diagnoses before accurate identification, if it occurs at all (Zimmerman et al., 2005). The internalized nature of symptoms creates assessment challenges that traditional diagnostic tools and clinical interview techniques may miss, while the high-functioning presentation can mask the severity of internal distress and interpersonal difficulties.

Clinical training programs historically emphasize crisis-oriented presentations of borderline personality disorder, leaving many mental health professionals unprepared to recognize or treat the subtle, internalized symptoms that characterize quiet BPD. This training gap contributes to underdiagnosis, inappropriate treatment approaches, and prolonged suffering for individuals and families seeking help (Paris, 2019).

Finding Therapists Who Recognize Internalized Patterns

Locating mental health professionals who understand quiet BPD requires strategic approach because standard therapist directories and referral sources often don't distinguish between professionals trained in different BPD presentations. The search process must balance finding appropriate expertise with practical considerations like location, insurance coverage, and availability.

Specialization identification involves looking for therapists with specific training in borderline personality disorder, dialectical behavior therapy, or trauma-informed approaches rather than general mental health practitioners. Professionals with DBT training often have better understanding of the emotional regulation challenges that underlie all BPD presentations, including internalized variants. Look for therapists who list specializations in personality disorders, emotional regulation difficulties, or high-functioning mental health presentations.

Training background research helps identify professionals with education and experience relevant to quiet BPD treatment. This includes therapists trained in evidence-based approaches like DBT, mentalization-based therapy, or schema therapy, all of which address the underlying patterns that characterize borderline presentations. Professionals with training in complex trauma or attachment-based therapies may also understand the developmental foundations of quiet BPD.

Interview strategies for potential therapists should focus on their understanding of internalized BPD presentations rather than their general experience with mental health treatment. Key questions include asking about their experience with high-functioning clients who struggle with internal emotional regulation, their understanding of different BPD presentations, and their approach to working with individuals whose external presentation doesn't match their internal experience.

Red flag identification helps avoid therapists whose approaches might be counterproductive for quiet BPD treatment. This includes therapists who focus primarily on behavioral modification without addressing emotional regulation, those who don't understand the complexity of BPD presentations, or professionals who emphasize pathology reduction rather than skill building and authentic emotional expression development.

Referral source utilization involves accessing professional networks that understand mental health complexity rather than relying on general referral services. This might include contacting DBT training programs for referrals, reaching out to local mental health organizations that specialize in personality disorders, or consulting with other mental health professionals who understand BPD presentations.

Geographic and accessibility considerations require balancing ideal therapeutic match with practical constraints like travel distance, session scheduling, and financial considerations. Telehealth options may expand access to specialized therapists who understand quiet BPD but aren't geographically accessible. However, ensure that any remote therapy options comply with relevant licensing and privacy regulations.

Treatment Modalities That Work Best

Research on borderline personality disorder treatment demonstrates that certain therapeutic approaches show superior effectiveness for addressing the core emotional regulation and interpersonal difficulties that characterize all BPD presentations, including quiet variants. Understanding these evidence-based approaches helps families advocate for appropriate treatment while avoiding less effective interventions.

Dialectical Behavior Therapy (DBT) remains the gold standard treatment for borderline personality disorder, with extensive research supporting its effectiveness for emotional regulation, distress tolerance, and interpersonal functioning improvements. DBT's skills-based approach addresses the core deficits underlying quiet BPD while teaching practical strategies for emotional expression and interpersonal effectiveness. The treatment's focus on accepting current functioning while building skills for change aligns well with quiet BPD presentations.

Mentalization-Based Therapy (MBT) specifically addresses the identity and interpersonal difficulties that characterize borderline presentations by focusing on developing the capacity to understand mental states underlying behavior. This approach proves particularly relevant for quiet BPD because individuals often struggle to identify and communicate their own emotional experiences while becoming hyperattuned to others' emotional states.

Schema Therapy addresses the underlying cognitive and emotional patterns that develop from early relational experiences, making it particularly relevant for quiet BPD presentations that often stem from complex developmental trauma. This approach focuses on identifying and modifying the maladaptive schemas that drive emotional suppression, perfectionism, and interpersonal difficulties.

Trauma-informed approaches recognize the role of developmental and relational trauma in creating the emotional regulation difficulties that characterize quiet BPD. These approaches focus on addressing trauma-related symptoms while building emotional regulation capacity and interpersonal skills. Eye Movement Desensitization and Reprocessing (EMDR) and other trauma-specific interventions may be integrated into treatment.

Cognitive Behavioral Therapy (CBT) adaptations can be effective for quiet BPD when modified to address emotional suppression patterns and perfectionist thinking styles. Standard CBT approaches may need adaptation to avoid reinforcing emotional control mechanisms while building capacity for authentic emotional expression and realistic thinking patterns.

Acceptance and Commitment Therapy (ACT) focuses on developing psychological flexibility and values-based living, which can address the rigidity and emotional avoidance that characterize quiet BPD presentations. ACT's emphasis on accepting difficult emotions while pursuing meaningful activities aligns with recovery goals for internalized BPD presentations.

How to Be an Effective Advocate

Advocacy for appropriate mental health treatment requires understanding both the mental health system and the specific challenges created by quiet BPD presentations. Effective advocacy balances respect for professional expertise with persistence in obtaining appropriate recognition and treatment.

Documentation strategies involve keeping detailed records of symptoms, treatment history, and functional impacts that can help professionals understand the severity and complexity of quiet BPD presentations. This includes documenting patterns over time, noting the disconnect between external functioning and internal experience, and tracking responses to different treatment approaches.

Communication approaches with mental health professionals require balancing education about quiet BPD with respect for professional expertise. This might involve sharing research about internalized BPD presentations, providing specific examples of symptoms and their impact, and asking direct questions about the professional's understanding of different BPD presentations.

Second opinion utilization becomes important when initial assessments don't capture the complexity of quiet BPD presentations or when treatment approaches aren't addressing underlying issues effectively. Seeking evaluation from professionals with specific BPD expertise can provide different perspectives and treatment recommendations.

Treatment goal clarification ensures that therapeutic interventions address the core issues underlying quiet BPD rather than focusing solely on surface symptoms like anxiety or depression. This includes advocating for treatment that addresses emotional regulation, authentic emotional expression, and interpersonal effectiveness rather than symptom management alone.

Family involvement coordination helps ensure that family education and support align with professional treatment approaches while maintaining appropriate boundaries. This might involve requesting family sessions to coordinate support strategies, asking for guidance about helpful family responses, and ensuring that family interventions support rather than undermine therapeutic goals.

Progress monitoring involves working collaboratively with mental health professionals to track meaningful improvements in emotional regulation, authentic expression, and interpersonal functioning rather than focusing solely on symptom reduction or external functioning measures.

Insurance and Accessibility Challenges

Mental health treatment for quiet BPD often faces unique insurance and accessibility barriers because the condition may not be immediately apparent during brief assessments, while evidence-based treatments may require longer-term intervention than insurance companies typically approve for initial treatment requests.

Insurance navigation strategies require understanding how mental health benefits apply to personality disorder treatment and advocating for coverage of evidence-based approaches. This includes understanding the difference between medical necessity criteria for different types of treatment, knowing how to appeal coverage denials, and accessing resources for insurance advocacy and support.

Prior authorization management for specialized treatments like DBT may require providing documentation about previous treatment attempts, evidence of medical necessity, and information about the specific approach being requested. Working with mental health professionals to provide compelling justification for specialized treatment can improve approval rates.

Alternative funding exploration might be necessary when insurance coverage is insufficient for appropriate treatment. This includes investigating sliding-scale fee options, community mental health resources, training clinics that offer reduced-cost services, and grant or scholarship programs for mental health treatment.

Access barrier problem-solving addresses practical challenges like transportation, scheduling, childcare, or work scheduling that can interfere with consistent treatment participation. Creative solutions might include telehealth options, flexible scheduling, or coordination with family members or support systems to address practical barriers.

Community resource utilization supplements professional treatment with peer support, educational programs, and skill-building opportunities that support recovery goals. This might include DBT skills groups, support groups for families affected by mental health conditions, or educational workshops about emotional regulation and interpersonal effectiveness.

Documentation for continued care ensures that treatment progress and ongoing needs are clearly documented to support continued insurance coverage and appropriate care transitions. This includes maintaining records of treatment goals, progress indicators, and ongoing treatment needs that justify continued professional intervention.

Coordinating Professional and Family Support

Effective treatment for quiet BPD requires coordination between professional interventions and family support to ensure that all efforts align toward common goals while maintaining appropriate boundaries between professional and family roles.

Treatment team communication establishes clear channels for sharing information between family members and mental health professionals while respecting privacy boundaries and therapeutic relationships. This might involve periodic family sessions, written progress updates, or consultation about family support strategies that complement professional treatment.

Role clarification helps family members understand their appropriate role in supporting recovery while avoiding attempts to serve as amateur therapists or treatment coordinators. This includes understanding the difference between supportive family responses and therapeutic interventions, maintaining focus on family relationship improvements rather than symptom management.

Crisis intervention coordination ensures that family responses during difficult periods align with professional crisis management plans and don't interfere with therapeutic goals. This includes understanding when to contact mental health professionals, how to provide appropriate support during crisis periods, and how to maintain safety while supporting professional intervention.

Progress celebration involves recognizing and acknowledging improvements in ways that support continued growth while maintaining realistic expectations about recovery timelines and processes. This includes celebrating increases in authentic emotional expression, improvements in interpersonal relationships, and development of emotional regulation skills.

Long-term planning coordinates professional treatment goals with family support strategies to create comprehensive approaches to recovery that can be sustained over time. This includes understanding how family support can continue to promote recovery as professional treatment intensity changes and ensuring that family members have ongoing resources and support for their own well-being.

The integration of professional treatment with family understanding and support creates the optimal conditions for recovery from quiet BPD. Understanding how to access appropriate professional help while maintaining effective family support provides the foundation for sustained improvement and family well-being. The next step involves developing long-term strategies for hope and recovery that acknowledge both the challenges and possibilities inherent in quiet BPD presentations.

Chapter 10: The Recovery Journey

Longitudinal research on borderline personality disorder recovery indicates that improvement occurs gradually over years rather than months, with studies showing that 85-88% of individuals achieve sustained remission within 10-15 years of appropriate treatment (Zanarini et al., 2010). However, recovery patterns for quiet BPD presentations differ significantly from classic presentations, involving subtle internal changes that may not be immediately apparent to outside observers or even to the individuals themselves. The internalized nature of symptoms means that early recovery often involves increased emotional awareness and expression that can initially feel destabilizing rather than improving.

Clinical observations reveal that quiet BPD recovery requires redefining success metrics beyond symptom reduction to include authenticity, emotional expression capacity, and genuine interpersonal connection. Traditional outcome measures focusing on crisis reduction, hospitalization avoidance, or behavioral stability may miss the meaningful internal changes that characterize recovery from internalized presentations (Gunderson et al., 2011).

What Recovery Looks Like with Quiet BPD

Recovery from quiet BPD involves fundamental shifts in how individuals relate to their emotions, themselves, and others, but these changes often occur beneath the surface of observable behavior. Unlike classic BPD recovery, which may involve obvious reductions in dramatic behaviors or crisis episodes, quiet BPD recovery manifests through subtle increases in authenticity, emotional expression, and interpersonal genuineness that family members must learn to recognize and celebrate.

Emotional expression expansion represents one of the most significant recovery indicators for quiet BPD. Early recovery often involves individuals beginning to express previously suppressed emotions, which can initially appear as increased negativity, criticism, or emotional instability. Family members may notice their loved one seems more irritable, sad, or anxious than before treatment, not recognizing that this emotional expression actually represents progress toward authentic functioning.

Perfectionism relaxation occurs gradually as individuals develop tolerance for imperfection in themselves and their environment. This might manifest as decreased cleaning compulsions, ability to leave projects unfinished, or reduced anxiety about making mistakes. Family members may notice their loved one seems less driven or motivated, not recognizing that this change represents healthy boundary setting rather than laziness or depression.

Interpersonal authenticity development involves gradual increases in honest communication, direct expression of needs, and willingness to engage in healthy conflict. Individuals may begin expressing disagreement, setting boundaries, or declining requests that they previously would have accepted automatically. Family members might initially experience this as their loved one becoming more difficult or demanding rather than recognizing it as healthy assertiveness development.

Identity clarification progresses slowly as individuals develop clearer sense of their own preferences, values, and goals independent of others' expectations. This might involve changes in career direction, relationship choices, or lifestyle preferences that can concern family members who have become accustomed to their loved one's adaptability and people-pleasing behaviors.

Emotional regulation improvements in quiet BPD recovery often involve increased emotional expression rather than increased emotional control. Individuals may appear more emotionally variable as they learn to experience and express feelings they previously suppressed. This can include appropriate anger expression, sadness about losses, or excitement about achievements that was previously muted.

Relationship pattern changes involve shifts toward more balanced, reciprocal interpersonal connections. Individuals may become less available for constant emotional caretaking of others while simultaneously becoming more willing to ask for support themselves. These changes can disrupt established family dynamics and may initially create conflict or discomfort.

Celebrating Small Victories and Internal Progress

Recognition and celebration of quiet BPD recovery progress requires developing new metrics for success that account for internal changes rather than focusing solely on external behavioral improvements. Family members must learn to identify and acknowledge subtle shifts that represent significant internal growth.

Emotional expression milestones deserve recognition even when they involve negative emotions or appear to create temporary family disruption. Celebrating when someone expresses anger directly rather than suppressing it, acknowledges sadness rather than maintaining artificial positivity, or shares anxiety rather than suffering silently validates their movement toward authentic emotional functioning.

Boundary setting victories require recognition even when family members are on the receiving end of newly established limits. When someone with quiet BPD begins saying no to requests, expressing preferences about activities, or declining to take on others' emotional problems, these behaviors represent significant progress toward healthy independence and self-advocacy.

Authenticity increases in daily interactions merit acknowledgment even when they involve admitting weaknesses, expressing needs, or revealing imperfections. Family members can celebrate when their loved one admits they don't know something, asks for help, or acknowledges making mistakes rather than maintaining their previous facade of competence and control.

Self-advocacy developments deserve recognition when individuals begin expressing their needs, preferences, or concerns directly rather than expecting others to guess or intuitively meet their requirements. This might involve stating food preferences, requesting schedule changes, or expressing feelings about family decisions that affect them.

Progress in therapy participation includes willingness to engage in treatment, increased openness with mental health professionals, and application of therapeutic skills in daily life. Family members can acknowledge their loved one's courage in pursuing treatment, consistency in attendance, or attempts to practice new skills even when these attempts aren't immediately successful.

Relationship risk-taking involves increased willingness to be vulnerable, express authentic emotions, or engage in honest communication despite fear of rejection or abandonment. Family members can celebrate when their loved one shares concerns, expresses disagreement, or reveals struggles rather than maintaining their previous emotional distance.

Relapse and Setbacks as Part of Healing

Recovery from quiet BPD rarely follows a linear progression, with setbacks and temporary returns to emotional suppression or perfectionist patterns being normal parts of the healing process rather than indicators of treatment failure. Understanding the nature and function of setbacks helps families respond supportively rather than with disappointment or renewed attempts to manage their loved one's symptoms.

Stress-triggered regressions commonly occur during periods of increased life stress, major transitions, or interpersonal conflicts when individuals temporarily revert to familiar coping mechanisms of emotional suppression and perfectionist control. These regressions serve protective functions and typically resolve as stress levels decrease and individuals regain access to newer coping skills.

Emotional overwhelm responses may temporarily cause individuals to return to emotional suppression when they encounter feelings that exceed their current regulation capacity. Rather than indicating treatment failure, these responses often reflect the individual's wisdom in protecting themselves from emotional experiences they're not yet equipped to handle effectively.

Anniversary reactions around significant dates, trauma reminders, or family events can trigger temporary increases in emotional suppression or perfectionist behaviors as protective responses to vulnerability. These reactions often decrease with experience and continued therapeutic work but may recur periodically throughout recovery.

Interpersonal stress responses during family conflicts, relationship changes, or social challenges may cause temporary returns to people-pleasing behaviors or emotional withdrawal as protective mechanisms. These responses often resolve as interpersonal stress decreases and individuals practice applying their developing skills to challenging situations.

Treatment resistance periods may occur when individuals become overwhelmed by the pace of change or frightened by increasing emotional awareness and expression. Temporary resistance to therapy, skill practice, or emotional expression often precedes periods of significant growth and integration.

Perfectionism resuregence during achievement-oriented situations, performance evaluations, or competitive environments may temporarily increase as individuals encounter situations that trigger their core fears of criticism or failure. These responses typically decrease as individuals gain experience managing performance anxiety with their developing skills.

Long-Term Relationship Strategies

Sustainable family relationships with quiet BPD require ongoing adaptation as recovery progresses and family dynamics shift in response to increased authenticity and emotional expression. Long-term strategies focus on maintaining supportive connections while allowing for continued growth and change.

Relationship expectation adjustments acknowledge that recovery changes the individual and therefore changes family relationships in ways that may require grieving previous dynamics while celebrating healthier patterns. Family members may need to adjust expectations about emotional availability, role responsibilities, and interaction styles as their loved one develops greater authenticity.

Communication pattern evolution involves family members adapting to increased directness, emotional expression, and boundary setting from their loved one while maintaining their own healthy communication practices. This might require learning to respond to conflict constructively, supporting emotional expression without trying to fix problems, and accepting changed relationship dynamics.

Boundary respect development requires family members to honor their loved one's increasing self-advocacy and limit-setting while maintaining their own healthy boundaries. This balance prevents either excessive accommodation that enables continued people-pleasing or rigid responses that punish healthy assertiveness development.

Conflict navigation skills become essential as increased authenticity may initially create more obvious disagreements and interpersonal friction. Family members need skills for engaging in healthy conflict resolution, managing their own emotional responses to disagreement, and supporting their loved one's developing conflict tolerance.

Growth space maintenance involves providing room for continued change and development rather than becoming attached to specific improvements or expecting recovery to reach a static endpoint. This includes accepting that their loved one may continue changing throughout recovery and that family relationships may continue requiring adaptation.

Professional support coordination helps families understand how to support ongoing recovery while maintaining appropriate boundaries around therapeutic work. This includes knowing when to encourage professional help, how to support treatment compliance, and when to step back and allow professional relationships to address specific recovery challenges.

Family Adaptation Throughout Recovery

Family systems must adapt continuously throughout the recovery process as increased authenticity and emotional expression from the individual with quiet BPD creates changes in family dynamics, role distributions, and communication patterns. These adaptations require patience, flexibility, and often professional guidance.

Role redistribution may be necessary as the individual with quiet BPD develops healthier boundaries and authentic self-expression that changes their previous family role. Family members who have taken on excessive emotional caretaking or decision-making responsibilities may need to gradually return these functions while supporting their loved one's developing independence.

Emotional system rebalancing occurs as the individual begins expressing previously suppressed emotions, potentially changing family emotional dynamics significantly. Family members may need to learn new ways of responding to emotional expression, managing their own reactions to increased authenticity, and maintaining their emotional regulation during family adjustment periods.

Communication system upgrades become necessary as increased directness and authenticity require more sophisticated family communication skills. This includes learning to respond to honest feedback, managing conflict constructively, and supporting emotional expression while maintaining healthy boundaries and family functioning.

Expectation recalibration involves adjusting family expectations about emotional availability, social participation, and role responsibilities as recovery progresses. This prevents disappointment when recovery doesn't match family expectations while celebrating actual improvements and changes.

Professional boundary maintenance helps families continue supporting recovery while respecting therapeutic relationships and avoiding overstepping appropriate family roles. This includes understanding when to encourage professional help versus providing family support and maintaining confidence in treatment processes even when progress seems slow.

Recovery Timeline Realities

Understanding realistic recovery timelines helps families maintain hope and persistence while avoiding frustration with the gradual pace of change characteristic of quiet BPD improvement. Recovery occurs over years rather than months, with different aspects improving at different rates.

Early recovery phases (first 6-18 months) often involve increased emotional awareness and expression that may initially appear destabilizing rather than improving. Family members need patience during this phase as their loved one learns to experience and express previously suppressed emotions while developing new coping mechanisms.

Skill development periods (months 6-36) focus on building emotional regulation, interpersonal effectiveness, and distress tolerance abilities through consistent practice and application. Progress during this phase may be subtle and require careful attention to recognize improvements in emotional management and relationship functioning.

Integration phases (years 2-5) involve applying developing skills to increasingly complex life situations while maintaining gains and continuing growth. Family members may notice their loved one handling stress more effectively, maintaining more authentic relationships, and demonstrating increased resilience during challenging periods.

Maintenance and growth (ongoing) recognizes that recovery from quiet BPD involves continued development rather than reaching a fixed endpoint. Individuals may continue developing emotional expression, authenticity, and relationship skills throughout their lives while maintaining their core improvements.

Building Hope for the Future

Recovery from quiet BPD offers genuine hope for increased authenticity, emotional connection, and life satisfaction despite the challenges involved in the healing process. Understanding the possibilities and maintaining realistic expectations helps families support long-term recovery while celebrating meaningful progress.

Quality of life improvements in recovered individuals include increased emotional awareness and expression, more authentic relationships, greater life satisfaction, and improved capacity for handling normal life stresses. These improvements often exceed pre-illness functioning as individuals develop emotional skills that many people never learn.

Relationship enhancement through recovery often results in deeper, more genuine connections as individuals become capable of authentic emotional expression and reciprocal interpersonal relationships. Family relationships frequently improve significantly as emotional suppression decreases and honest communication increases.

Personal growth acceleration often occurs during recovery as individuals develop emotional awareness and expression capabilities that support continued learning and development throughout life. Many individuals report that recovery from quiet BPD creates opportunities for personal growth and self-discovery that enhance their lives in unexpected ways.

Contribution capacity increases as emotional regulation improves and authenticity develops, allowing individuals to contribute meaningfully to family, work, and community relationships. Recovery often enables individuals to use their sensitivity and emotional awareness in ways that benefit others while maintaining their own well-being.

The recovery journey from quiet BPD requires patience, understanding, and faith in the possibility of change despite the gradual and sometimes invisible nature of progress. Understanding what recovery looks like and how families can support this process creates the foundation for building resilience and meaning throughout the healing journey.

Chapter 11: Building Resilience Together

Research on family resilience in mental health contexts demonstrates that families who develop understanding, meaning-making capacity, and adaptive coping strategies show significantly better long-term outcomes than those who focus solely on symptom management or crisis response (Walsh, 2016). Studies indicate that families affected by quiet BPD presentations often develop unique strengths including enhanced emotional awareness, improved communication skills, and deeper capacity for empathy and authentic connection when they successfully navigate the challenges together.

Clinical observations reveal that the invisible nature of quiet BPD symptoms can initially fragment family understanding and create isolation, but families who develop frameworks for recognizing and responding to internalized struggles often emerge with stronger bonds and more sophisticated interpersonal skills than families who never face these challenges (Boss, 2006).

Strengthening Family Bonds Through Understanding

Deep understanding of quiet BPD's impact on family relationships creates opportunities for enhanced connection and intimacy that may not have been possible without facing these challenges together. The process of learning to recognize and respond to internal struggles develops family capacities for emotional awareness and authentic communication that strengthen relationships beyond symptom management.

Emotional literacy development throughout the family system occurs as members learn to recognize subtle emotional cues, understand the complexity of internal experiences, and communicate about feelings with greater sophistication. Family members often report that learning to understand quiet BPD enhances their ability to recognize and respond to their own and others' emotional needs in all relationships.

Compassion expansion develops as family members gain insight into the internal struggle that accompanies quiet BPD presentations. Understanding the effort required to maintain external functioning despite internal chaos often creates profound appreciation for their loved one's strength while developing patience for the recovery process and its inherent challenges.

Communication depth increases as families learn to look beyond surface presentations to understand underlying experiences and needs. This skill often translates to improved communication in all family relationships as members become more skilled at authentic expression and empathetic listening rather than assuming surface appearances reflect complete reality.

Patience and persistence cultivation occurs as families learn to support gradual change processes rather than expecting immediate improvements or dramatic transformations. These skills prove valuable for all family challenges and relationship development throughout life, creating more sustainable and realistic approaches to personal growth and relationship maintenance.

Authenticity appreciation develops as families learn to value genuine emotional expression over artificial harmony or perfect presentations. This often leads to increased honesty and emotional intimacy throughout the family system as members feel safer expressing their true experiences rather than maintaining facades.

Problem-solving sophistication increases as families learn to address complex, subtle challenges that don't have obvious solutions or quick fixes. These enhanced problem-solving capabilities often improve family functioning in multiple areas as members become more skilled at addressing nuanced interpersonal issues.

Creating Meaning from the Struggle

Finding purpose and significance in the challenges created by quiet BPD helps families maintain hope and motivation while transforming suffering into opportunities for growth, connection, and contribution. Meaning-making processes prevent families from becoming defined by mental health challenges while creating frameworks for understanding their experiences positively.

Growth narrative development involves framing the family's experience with quiet BPD as a journey of learning, development, and enhanced capacity rather than simply an unfortunate circumstance to endure. This perspective highlights the skills, understanding, and resilience that emerge from successfully navigating these challenges together.

Strength identification focuses on recognizing the capabilities and resources that families develop through their experience with quiet BPD. These might include enhanced emotional awareness, improved communication skills, increased patience and empathy, or greater appreciation for authenticity and genuine connection in relationships.

Purpose discovery involves identifying ways that the family's experience can contribute to others facing similar challenges or enhance their capacity to support people in their community. Many families find meaning through sharing their experiences, supporting other families, or using their enhanced emotional skills in professional or volunteer contexts.

Legacy creation considers how the family's journey through quiet BPD challenges creates lasting positive impacts for future generations. This might involve passing on enhanced emotional literacy skills, modeling authentic communication patterns, or creating family traditions that support emotional expression and genuine connection.

Wisdom integration involves incorporating the insights gained through their experience into family values, decision-making processes, and approach to future challenges. This wisdom often includes appreciation for emotional complexity, understanding of the difference between surface appearances and underlying experiences, and skills for supporting each other through difficult periods.

Connection deepening recognizes how facing challenges together can create bonds and intimacy that might not have developed otherwise. Many families report that their experience with quiet BPD, while difficult, ultimately created closer relationships and deeper understanding among family members.

Developing Compassion for the Invisible Battle

Understanding the internal struggle that characterizes quiet BPD helps family members develop profound compassion not only for their loved one but also for others who face invisible challenges. This compassion becomes a source of meaning and connection that extends beyond the immediate family situation.

Invisible struggle recognition develops as family members learn to identify signs of internal distress in their loved one and begin recognizing similar patterns in others they encounter. This awareness often creates increased sensitivity to the reality that many people face significant internal challenges that aren't visible to outside observers.

Judgment reduction occurs naturally as family members gain understanding of how internal experiences can differ dramatically from external presentations. This understanding often leads to decreased criticism of others and increased curiosity about underlying experiences rather than making assumptions based on surface behaviors.

Empathy expansion develops through direct experience with loving someone whose internal experience differs significantly from their external presentation. This empathy often extends to other situations where surface appearances may mask underlying struggles, creating more compassionate responses to human complexity.

Advocacy motivation emerges as families understand how invisible struggles can be misunderstood or dismissed by others who lack awareness. Many family members become advocates for mental health understanding, emotional authenticity, or support for people facing invisible challenges.

Tolerance for complexity increases as families learn that human experiences often involve contradictions, gradual change processes, and situations that don't have simple explanations or quick solutions. This tolerance serves families well in multiple life contexts beyond mental health challenges.

Appreciation for effort develops as family members understand the energy required to maintain functioning despite internal struggles. This appreciation often extends to recognizing and valuing effort over outcomes in many life situations, creating more supportive and encouraging family environments.

Tools for Ongoing Growth

Building family resilience requires developing sustainable practices and approaches that support continued growth and adaptation rather than simply crisis management or symptom control. These tools help families maintain their gains while continuing to develop their capacity for authentic connection and mutual support.

Regular family reflection practices create ongoing opportunities for family members to share their experiences, celebrate progress, and address emerging challenges together. This might involve monthly family meetings, annual family retreats, or regular check-ins that maintain open communication and mutual support.

Skill practice maintenance involves continuing to develop and refine the communication, emotional regulation, and problem-solving skills that support family functioning. This includes ongoing practice of validation techniques, boundary setting, and authentic expression that maintain and enhance family relationship quality.

Growth mindset cultivation maintains focus on continued learning and development rather than achieving fixed endpoints or perfect family functioning. This perspective supports ongoing adaptation to changing needs and circumstances while maintaining hope and motivation for continued improvement.

Stress management systems provide families with reliable approaches for managing future challenges and difficult periods. These systems include both individual and family strategies for maintaining emotional regulation, communication effectiveness, and mutual support during stressful times.

External support maintenance ensures that families continue to access professional support, peer connections, and community resources that support their ongoing growth and development. This includes maintaining therapeutic relationships as needed, participating in support groups, and accessing educational resources that enhance understanding.

Celebration and gratitude practices help families maintain awareness of their progress, strengths, and positive experiences while avoiding becoming overwhelmed by ongoing challenges. Regular celebration of progress and expression of gratitude for family connections maintain positive perspectives and motivation.

Building on Family Strengths

Every family develops unique strengths and capabilities through their experience with quiet BPD that can be identified, celebrated, and built upon for continued growth and contribution. Recognizing these strengths prevents families from focusing solely on challenges while creating foundations for ongoing development.

Communication strength enhancement builds on the sophisticated communication skills that many families develop through learning to recognize and respond to subtle emotional cues and internalized struggles. These skills often exceed those of families who haven't faced similar challenges and can be further developed for enhanced family functioning.

Emotional intelligence development capitalizes on the heightened emotional awareness that families often develop through their experience with quiet BPD. This awareness can be cultivated further through continued learning about emotional literacy, regulation techniques, and interpersonal effectiveness skills.

Problem-solving capability expansion builds on the complex problem-solving skills that families develop through addressing challenges that don't have obvious solutions or quick fixes. These capabilities can be applied to other family challenges and life situations while continuing to develop through practice and education.

Resilience and persistence strengthening capitalizes on the endurance and flexibility that families develop through supporting long-term recovery processes. These strengths can be enhanced through continued stress management education, resilience building practices, and community connection.

Empathy and compassion deepening builds on the enhanced capacity for understanding and supporting others that many families develop through their experience. These capabilities can be cultivated through volunteer work, peer support activities, or professional development that utilizes their enhanced emotional skills.

Creating Family Legacy

The experience of facing and successfully managing quiet BPD challenges creates opportunities for families to develop lasting positive impacts that extend beyond their immediate situation. This legacy perspective transforms current challenges into foundations for future contribution and meaning.

Intergenerational skill transmission involves consciously passing on the enhanced emotional literacy, communication skills, and resilience capabilities that develop through the family's experience. This creates lasting positive impacts for future generations while ensuring that current challenges contribute to long-term family strengths.

Community contribution development utilizes the family's enhanced understanding and skills to support others facing similar challenges. This might involve sharing experiences, providing peer support, advocating for mental health awareness, or contributing to educational and support resources for other families.

Professional enhancement opportunities recognize how the skills and understanding developed through family experience with quiet BPD can enhance career capabilities in fields involving human service, education, healthcare, or interpersonal relationships. Many family members find that their experience creates valuable perspectives and skills for professional contribution.

Advocacy and awareness promotion involves using the family's experience to increase understanding of quiet BPD presentations and reduce stigma around invisible mental health challenges. This contribution helps create more supportive environments for others facing similar struggles while creating meaning from the family's experience.

Model development involves consciously creating examples of how families can successfully support recovery while maintaining healthy relationships and individual well-being. This modeling contributes to community understanding while creating frameworks that other families can adapt for their own situations.

Sustaining Hope and Motivation

Long-term resilience building requires maintaining hope and motivation through inevitable challenges and setbacks while celebrating progress and maintaining vision for continued growth and contribution. This sustainability prevents burnout while supporting continued family development.

Vision maintenance involves keeping focus on long-term goals for family connection, individual growth, and contribution rather than becoming overwhelmed by immediate challenges or setbacks. This perspective maintains motivation while providing direction for continued development efforts.

Progress recognition systems help families notice and celebrate incremental improvements that might otherwise go unrecognized. This includes tracking emotional regulation improvements, communication enhancements, relationship quality increases, and individual growth achievements that validate ongoing efforts.

Challenge reframing maintains perspective on difficulties as opportunities for continued learning and growth rather than threats to family stability or indicators of failure. This reframing maintains resilience while supporting continued problem-solving efforts and skill development.

Support system utilization ensures that families continue accessing external resources, professional support, and peer connections that maintain their energy and motivation for continued growth. This prevents isolation while providing encouragement and practical assistance.

Meaning-making maintenance involves regularly revisiting and updating the family's understanding of how their experience contributes to their growth, connection, and ability to contribute to others. This meaning-making prevents the experience from becoming simply a burden while maintaining awareness of its positive impacts.

The journey of building resilience together transforms the challenges created by quiet BPD into opportunities for profound family growth, enhanced connection, and meaningful contribution to others facing similar struggles. This transformation creates lasting positive impacts that extend far beyond the immediate situation while providing hope and direction for continued development.

Chapter 12: Resources and Next Steps

Research on resource utilization for families affected by borderline personality disorder indicates that access to appropriate support, education, and professional services significantly improves both individual recovery outcomes and family functioning (Hoffman & Fruzzetti, 2007). However, families dealing with quiet BPD presentations face unique challenges in resource identification because many services focus on crisis intervention and obvious behavioral symptoms rather than addressing the subtle, internalized struggles that characterize these presentations.

Clinical experience demonstrates that successful long-term management of quiet BPD requires coordinated access to multiple types of resources including specialized mental health services, family education and support, peer connections, and ongoing educational materials that address the specific challenges of internalized borderline presentations (Gunderson, 2008).

Comprehensive Resource Directory

Building an effective support system for quiet BPD requires identifying and accessing multiple types of resources that address different aspects of the condition and its impact on family functioning. This comprehensive approach ensures that families have access to professional treatment, peer support, educational materials, and crisis resources when needed.

Professional treatment resources form the foundation of effective quiet BPD management, requiring identification of mental health professionals who understand internalized presentations and can provide appropriate evidence-based interventions. Key professional resources include:

Dialectical Behavior Therapy (DBT) providers who offer individual therapy, skills groups, and consultation services specifically designed for borderline personality disorder treatment. Many DBT programs now recognize quiet presentations and adapt their approaches accordingly. Search for providers through the Behavioral Tech website, which maintains directories of DBT-trained professionals, or contact local training programs that may offer sliding-scale services.

Mentalization-Based Therapy (MBT) practitioners who specialize in helping individuals develop capacity for understanding mental states underlying behavior. This approach proves particularly valuable for quiet BPD presentations that involve identity confusion and interpersonal difficulties. The Anna Freud Centre website provides information about MBT training and certified practitioners.

Emergency and crisis resources provide essential support during periods when internal distress becomes unmanageable or when family members need immediate guidance about safety concerns:

National Suicide Prevention Lifeline (988) offers 24-hour crisis support, risk assessment, and local resource referrals for individuals experiencing suicidal thoughts or emotional crisis. The service provides specialized training for supporting individuals with personality disorders and understands the unique presentations of internalized distress.

Crisis Text Line (Text HOME to 741741) provides immediate support through text messaging for individuals who may find verbal communication difficult during emotional overwhelm. This service often appeals to individuals with quiet BPD who struggle with direct emotional expression but can communicate through writing.

Support Groups and Online Communities

Peer support provides unique benefits for families affected by quiet BPD because connecting with others who understand similar experiences reduces isolation while providing practical strategies and emotional validation that complement professional treatment.

Family support organizations offer education, support groups, and advocacy resources specifically designed for family members of individuals with mental health conditions:

National Education Alliance for Borderline Personality Disorder (NEA-BPD) provides family education programs, support groups, and educational materials specifically focused on borderline personality disorder. Their Family Connections program offers structured education and support for family members, with many groups now addressing quiet presentations specifically.

NAMI (National Alliance on Mental Illness) offers family support groups, educational programs, and advocacy resources for families affected by mental health conditions. While not specific to BPD, many NAMI programs address personality disorders and provide valuable support for family members navigating mental health challenges.

Online community resources provide accessible support for families who may not have local resources or who prefer digital connection options:

BPD Family support forums offer moderated online communities where family members can share experiences, ask questions, and receive support from others facing similar challenges. These communities often include specific sections for quiet BPD presentations and high-functioning presentations.

Reddit communities such as r/BPDlovedones and r/BPDfamily provide peer support and information sharing, though these require careful navigation to avoid purely venting-focused discussions that may increase rather than decrease family distress. Look for communities that emphasize support and skill-building rather than just complaint sharing.

Recommended Reading and Continuing Education

Educational resources help families develop deeper understanding of quiet BPD while providing practical strategies for ongoing support and relationship management. Continued learning supports long-term family adaptation and skill development.

Foundational books provide essential understanding of borderline personality disorder and evidence-based treatment approaches:

"I Hate You—Don't Leave Me" by Jerold Kreisman and Hal Straus offers accessible explanation of borderline personality disorder dynamics and family impact, with updated editions that address quiet presentations and high-functioning variants.

"The Essential Family Guide to Borderline Personality Disorder" by Randi Kreger provides practical strategies for family members, including communication techniques, boundary setting, and self-care approaches specifically designed for families affected by BPD.

Treatment-focused resources help families understand evidence-based interventions and how to support professional treatment:

"Skills Training Manual for Treating Borderline Personality Disorder" by Marsha Linehan provides detailed explanation of DBT skills that families can learn to support their own emotional regulation and communication effectiveness. While written for professionals, many sections offer valuable insights for family members.

"Mind Over Mood" by Dennis Greenberger and Christine Padesky teaches cognitive-behavioral strategies that complement professional treatment while providing practical tools for managing anxiety, depression, and emotional regulation challenges that affect family members.

Specialized quiet BPD resources address the unique challenges of internalized presentations:

"Quiet BPD: The Invisible Struggle" online resources provide specific information about recognizing and understanding internalized borderline presentations, though families should verify the credibility of online resources and supplement with professional guidance.

"High-Functioning Mental Health" educational materials help families understand how mental health conditions can coexist with external success and competence, providing frameworks for recognizing internal struggles that may not be immediately apparent.

Creating Your Family Action Plan

Developing a structured approach to managing quiet BPD in family context requires creating personalized plans that address your specific situation while incorporating evidence-based strategies and appropriate resources. This action plan provides direction while maintaining flexibility for changing needs and circumstances.

Assessment and goal setting forms the foundation of effective family action planning by identifying current challenges, available resources, and desired outcomes:

Family needs assessment involves honest evaluation of current family functioning, individual stress levels, and areas requiring improvement. This includes identifying specific challenges created by quiet BPD, assessing current coping strategies, and recognizing family strengths that can be built upon.

Goal prioritization focuses family efforts on the most important changes while avoiding overwhelming attempts to address everything simultaneously. Goals might include improving communication patterns, developing better crisis management strategies, enhancing individual self-care, or accessing appropriate professional treatment.

Resource identification and access ensures that families have appropriate support systems in place before crises occur:

Professional treatment coordination involves identifying and accessing mental health professionals who understand quiet BPD presentations while ensuring that family members have their own support resources as needed. This includes researching insurance coverage, identifying local providers, and establishing relationships before urgent needs arise.

110

Support network development creates connections with other families, peer support resources, and educational programs that provide ongoing encouragement and practical guidance. This network should include both professional and peer resources that can provide different types of support as needs change.

Implementation strategies translate assessment and resource identification into practical daily actions and approaches:

Communication system implementation involves practicing the validation, boundary-setting, and authentic expression skills that support healthy family relationships while addressing quiet BPD challenges. This includes establishing regular family meeting times, practicing specific communication techniques, and creating safe spaces for emotional expression.

Crisis planning development creates structured approaches for managing periods of increased distress or family difficulty while maintaining safety and connection. Crisis plans should include early warning sign recognition, specific intervention strategies, professional resource activation, and family support coordination.

Action Plan Components

Effective family action plans include specific, measurable components that can be implemented, monitored, and adjusted as circumstances change. These components address immediate needs while building capacity for long-term success.

Individual development plans ensure that each family member has personal support and growth strategies:

Personal skill building focuses on developing emotional regulation, stress management, and communication capabilities that support individual well-being while enhancing capacity to support family relationships. This includes identifying specific skills to develop, creating practice schedules, and accessing appropriate learning resources.

Self-care maintenance establishes sustainable approaches to maintaining physical, emotional, and social well-being that prevent caregiver burnout while supporting long-term family functioning. Self-care plans should include regular activities, support relationships, and personal interests that restore rather than drain individual energy.

Family system interventions address relationship patterns and communication dynamics that support overall family functioning:

Communication pattern modification involves implementing specific changes to family interaction styles that promote authenticity while maintaining emotional safety for all family members. This includes practicing validation techniques, establishing conflict resolution procedures, and creating opportunities for positive family connection.

Boundary establishment creates clear expectations about individual responsibilities, emotional availability, and family roles that support healthy independence while maintaining appropriate connection and support. Boundary plans should address both individual and family needs while allowing for adaptation as circumstances change.

Professional support integration coordinates family efforts with professional treatment and support services:

Treatment support coordination ensures that family responses complement rather than conflict with professional interventions while maintaining appropriate boundaries around therapeutic relationships. This includes understanding treatment goals, supporting treatment compliance, and accessing family education resources that align with professional recommendations.

Progress monitoring systems track meaningful improvements in family functioning, individual well-being, and quiet BPD symptoms while celebrating achievements and identifying areas requiring continued attention. Monitoring should focus on long-term trends rather than daily variations while maintaining realistic expectations about recovery timelines.

Implementation Timeline

Creating realistic timelines for family action plan implementation prevents overwhelming expectations while ensuring steady progress toward identified goals. Timelines should account for the gradual nature of change in quiet BPD situations while maintaining motivation and direction.

Immediate priorities (first 1-3 months) focus on stabilizing current situations and establishing foundational resources:

Crisis safety planning ensures that families have appropriate resources and procedures in place for managing periods of increased distress or safety concerns. This includes identifying emergency contacts, understanding when to seek professional help, and establishing family communication procedures during difficult periods.

Basic resource identification involves researching and contacting professional treatment providers, family support resources, and educational materials that address quiet BPD presentations. This foundation provides direction for continued resource development and access.

Short-term goals (3-12 months) build on immediate stabilization efforts while developing enhanced family functioning:

Communication skill implementation involves practicing and refining validation, boundary-setting, and authentic expression techniques that improve family relationships while supporting quiet BPD recovery. Skill development requires consistent practice and patience as family members learn new interaction patterns.

Support system development expands family access to peer support, educational resources, and professional services that provide ongoing encouragement and practical guidance. Support systems should include both crisis resources and ongoing maintenance support that prevents isolation and provides perspective.

Long-term development (1-3 years and beyond) focuses on maintaining gains while continuing growth and adaptation:

Family resilience building creates sustainable patterns that support continued family growth and adaptation while maintaining the gains achieved through earlier interventions. Resilience building includes developing meaning-making capacity, maintaining hope during challenges, and creating positive family legacies.

Community contribution development utilizes family experience and enhanced capabilities to support others facing similar challenges while creating meaning and purpose from their own struggles. Contribution activities might include peer support, advocacy work, or professional development that utilizes their enhanced understanding and skills.

The comprehensive resource directory and family action planning process provides practical direction for accessing support while creating individualized approaches that address specific family needs and circumstances. These resources form the foundation for long-term success in managing quiet BPD while building stronger, more authentic family relationships.

Appendix A: Quick Reference Guides

Crisis Intervention Flowchart

Assess Immediate Safety

- Is there immediate danger to self or others?

- Are there specific plans or means for self-harm?

- Is the person responsive and able to communicate?

If immediate danger exists:

- Call 911 or emergency services

- Do not leave the person alone

- Remove any dangerous items if safely possible

- Stay calm and supportive while waiting for help

If no immediate danger:

- Use calming communication techniques

- Validate their emotional experience

- Avoid minimizing or dismissing their feelings

- Offer specific, practical support

Next Steps:

- Contact mental health professional if available

- Use crisis text line (741741) or crisis hotline (988)

- Implement family crisis plan if established

- Follow up with professional support within 24 hours

Communication Do's and Don'ts

DO:

- Validate their internal experience
- Use "I" statements to express your feelings
- Give them time to process information
- Acknowledge their efforts and strengths
- Ask open-ended questions when appropriate
- Maintain calm tone and body language

DON'T:

- Assume you know how they're feeling
- Use absolute words like "always" or "never"
- Pressure for immediate emotional responses
- Minimize their experiences with phrases like "just relax"
- Take their emotional reactions personally
- Try to fix their problems immediately

Warning Signs Checklist

Early Warning Signs:

- Increased perfectionist behaviors
- Social withdrawal or emotional distance
- Changes in sleep or eating patterns
- Increased irritability or sensitivity
- Neglecting previously enjoyed activities
- Excessive focus on work or achievements

Escalating Concerns:

- Expressing feelings of hopelessness
- Significant changes in daily functioning
- Increased isolation from family and friends
- Talking about being a burden to others
- Giving away personal possessions
- Extreme mood swings or emotional numbness

Crisis Indicators:

- Direct or indirect threats of self-harm
- Specific plans for ending their life
- Engaging in dangerous or reckless behaviors
- Complete emotional shutdown or inability to respond
- Psychotic symptoms or loss of reality contact
- Substance abuse as coping mechanism

Emergency Contact Templates

Personal Emergency Contacts:

- Primary mental health provider: _____
- Backup therapist or crisis counselor: _____
- Trusted family member or friend: _____
- Medical doctor: _____

Crisis Resources:

- National Suicide Prevention Lifeline: 988
- Crisis Text Line: Text HOME to 741741

- Local emergency room: _____
- Local crisis intervention team: _____

Important Information to Share:

- Current medications and dosages
- Known triggers or warning signs
- Preferred hospital or treatment facility
- Insurance information and member ID
- Any advance directives or treatment preferences

Appendix B: Worksheets and Tools

Family Assessment Questionnaire

Communication Patterns (Rate 1-5, with 5 being most accurate):

1. Family members feel safe expressing their true feelings ___

2. We listen to each other without immediately trying to fix problems ___

3. Disagreements are handled respectfully and constructively ___

4. Everyone's needs and preferences are considered in family decisions ___

5. We can discuss difficult topics without major conflict ___

Emotional Climate:

1. Our home feels emotionally safe and supportive ___

2. Family members respect each other's need for space ___

3. We celebrate achievements and support each other during challenges ___

4. Stress and anxiety are managed effectively by family members ___

5. There's a balance between individual needs and family connection ___

Support and Understanding:

1. Family members understand quiet BPD and its impact ___

2. We have effective strategies for managing difficult periods ___

3. Everyone has access to individual support and self-care ___

4. We coordinate well with professional treatment providers ___

5. Our family has hope and positive vision for the future ___

Boundary-Setting Worksheet

Identify Your Limits:

- What behaviors are you no longer willing to accept?

- What responsibilities belong to you versus other family members?

- What support are you able to provide versus what feels overwhelming?

- What topics or situations trigger your own emotional overwhelm?

Communication Scripts:

- "I care about you, and I'm not able to [specific behavior]"

- "I want to support you, and I need to [specific boundary]"

- "This feels too overwhelming for me right now. Can we [alternative]?"

- "I'm here for you, and I also need to take care of myself by [specific action]"

Boundary Maintenance:

- How will you respond when boundaries are tested?

- What support do you need to maintain these limits?

- How will you communicate boundary changes if needed?

- What will you do if maintaining boundaries creates conflict?

Progress Tracking Tool

Weekly Observations (Track for 4-6 weeks):

Emotional Expression:

- Frequency of authentic emotional sharing: ___
- Comfort level with expressing needs directly: ___
- Ability to tolerate and express negative emotions: ___

Relationship Quality:

- Level of genuine connection during interactions: ___
- Frequency of meaningful conversations: ___
- Ability to resolve conflicts constructively: ___

Individual Functioning:

- Energy levels and overall well-being: ___
- Ability to maintain daily responsibilities: ___
- Engagement in personally meaningful activities: ___

Family System:

- Overall family harmony and cooperation: ___
- Effectiveness of family problem-solving: ___
- Mutual support during challenging periods: ___

Self-Care Planning Guide

Physical Self-Care:

- Regular exercise or movement activities: _____
- Adequate sleep schedule and routine: _____

- Nutritious eating habits and meal planning: _____

- Medical care and health maintenance: _____

Emotional Self-Care:

- Individual therapy or counseling support: _____

- Stress management and relaxation techniques: _____

- Creative outlets and personal interests: _____

- Spiritual or mindfulness practices: _____

Social Self-Care:

- Supportive friendships and social connections: _____

- Family relationships that provide mutual support: _____

- Community involvement or volunteer activities: _____

- Professional networks and work relationships: _____

Intellectual Self-Care:

- Learning opportunities and personal growth: _____

- Reading, education, or skill development: _____

- Problem-solving and decision-making support: _____

- Goal-setting and future planning activities: _____

Appendix C: Professional Resources

How to Find Qualified Therapists

Search Strategies:

1. Contact your insurance provider for in-network mental health professionals

2. Use Psychology Today's therapist finder with filters for BPD specialization

3. Search the Behavioral Tech website for DBT-trained providers

4. Contact local universities with psychology training programs

5. Ask current healthcare providers for referrals

Questions to Ask Potential Therapists:

- "What experience do you have treating borderline personality disorder?"

- "Are you familiar with quiet or high-functioning BPD presentations?"

- "What treatment approaches do you use for personality disorders?"

- "How do you involve family members in treatment planning?"

- "What is your approach to crisis situations and emergency contact?"

Red Flags to Avoid:

- Providers who claim they can "cure" personality disorders quickly

- Therapists who focus primarily on medication without therapy

- Professionals who seem unfamiliar with evidence-based BPD treatments

- Providers who make you feel judged or dismissed during initial consultation

- Therapists who don't maintain clear boundaries or professional standards

Questions to Ask Mental Health Providers

About Their Experience:

- How many individuals with BPD have you treated?

- What training do you have in personality disorder treatment?

- Are you familiar with the differences between quiet and classic BPD?

- How do you stay current with BPD research and treatment developments?

About Treatment Approach:

- What evidence-based treatments do you use for BPD?

- How long does treatment typically take?

- How do you measure progress and success?

- What role do family members play in your treatment approach?

About Practical Matters:

- What are your fees and payment policies?

- How do you handle insurance and billing?

- What is your availability for appointments and crisis contact?

- How do you coordinate with other healthcare providers?

Insurance Navigation Guide

Understanding Your Benefits:

1. Review your mental health coverage limits and requirements
2. Identify whether you need referrals for specialist care
3. Understand your deductible and copayment responsibilities
4. Learn about any pre-authorization requirements for treatment

Advocating for Coverage:

1. Document medical necessity for specialized treatment
2. Request written denials to appeal if coverage is rejected
3. Work with providers to submit appropriate diagnostic codes
4. Appeal coverage decisions with supporting documentation

Alternative Funding Options:

- Sliding scale fees at community mental health centers
- Training clinics at universities or professional schools
- Employee assistance programs through workplace benefits
- State-funded mental health services for qualifying individuals
- Nonprofit organizations offering mental health support

Treatment Center Directory

Specialized BPD Programs:

- McLean Hospital (Belmont, MA) - Residential and outpatient BPD programs
- Menninger Clinic (Houston, TX) - Adolescent and adult personality disorder treatment

- Sheppard Pratt (Baltimore, MD) - DBT programs and personality disorder services

- Three Springs (Huntsville, UT) - Residential treatment for young adults

DBT Training and Treatment Centers:

- Behavioral Tech (Seattle, WA) - Training and intensive DBT programs

- Cognitive and Behavioral Consultants (Westport, CT) - DBT and personality disorder treatment

- Houston DBT Institute (Houston, TX) - Training and clinical services

- Philadelphia DBT Center (Philadelphia, PA) - Individual and group DBT services

Online and Telehealth Resources:

- BetterHelp and similar platforms with BPD-specialized providers

- DBT online skills groups and educational programs

- Telehealth services specifically designed for personality disorder treatment

- Virtual family therapy and support programs

Crisis and Emergency Resources:

- National Suicide Prevention Lifeline: 988

- Crisis Text Line: Text HOME to 741741

- National Alliance on Mental Illness (NAMI): 1-800-950-NAMI

- Substance Abuse and Mental Health Services Administration: 1-800-662-4357

These appendices provide practical tools and resources that families can use immediately while building their long-term support systems and coping strategies. Regular reference to these materials helps maintain focus on evidence-based approaches while providing quick access to essential information during challenging periods.

References

Boss, P. (2006). Loss, trauma, and resilience: Therapeutic work with ambiguous loss. W. W. Norton & Company.

Carpenter, R. W., & Trull, T. J. (2013). Components of emotion dysregulation in borderline personality disorder: A review. Current Psychiatry Reports, 15(1), 335.

Carpenter, R. W., Wood, P. K., & Trull, T. J. (2016). Comorbidity of borderline personality disorder and lifetime substance use disorders in a nationally representative sample. Journal of Personality Disorders, 30(3), 336-350.

Crowell, S. E., Beauchaine, T. P., & Linehan, M. M. (2009). A biosocial developmental model of borderline personality: Elaborating and extending Linehan's theory. Psychological Bulletin, 135(3), 495-510.

Fonagy, P., Luyten, P., Moulton-Perkins, A., Lee, Y. W., Warren, F., Howard, S., ... & Lowyck, B. (2016). Development and validation of a self-report measure of mentalizing: The reflective functioning questionnaire. PLoS One, 11(7), e0158678.

Fossati, A., Krueger, R. F., Markon, K. E., Borroni, S., Maffei, C., & Somma, A. (2014). The personality inventory for DSM-5 brief form: Evidence for reliability and construct validity in a sample of community-dwelling Italian adults. Assessment, 21(4), 413-424.

Fruzzetti, A. E., & Fruzzetti, A. R. (2003). Borderline personality disorder. In D. K. Snyder & M. A. Whisman (Eds.), Treating difficult couples: Helping clients with coexisting mental and relationship disorders (pp. 235-260). Guilford Press.

Goodman, M., Carpenter, D., Tang, C. Y., Goldstein, K. E., Avedon, J., Fernandez, N., ... & Hazlett, E. A. (2014). Dialectical behavior therapy alters emotion regulation and amygdala activity in patients with borderline personality disorder. Journal of Psychiatric Research, 57, 108-116.

Gunderson, J. G. (2008). Borderline personality disorder: A clinical guide (2nd ed.). American Psychiatric Publishing.

Gunderson, J. G. (2009). Borderline personality disorder: A clinical guide (2nd ed.). American Psychiatric Publishing

Gunderson, J. G., Herpertz, S. C., Skodol, A. E., Torgersen, S., & Zanarini, M. C. (2018). Borderline personality disorder. Nature Reviews Disease Primers, 4, 18029

Gunderson, J. G., & Lyons-Ruth, K. (2008). BPD's interpersonal hypersensitivity phenotype: A gene-environment-developmental model. Journal of Personality Disorders, 22(1), 22-41.

Gunderson, J. G., Stout, R. L., McGlashan, T. H., Shea, M. T., Morey, L. C., Grilo, C. M., ... & Skodol, A. E. (2011). Ten-year course of borderline personality disorder: Psychopathology and function from the Collaborative Longitudinal Personality Disorders study. Archives of General Psychiatry, 68(8), 827-837.

Hazlett, E. A., Zhang, J., New, A. S., Zelmanova, Y., Goldstein, K. E., Haznedar, M. M., ... & Chu, K. W. (2012). Potentiated amygdala response to repeated emotional pictures in borderline personality disorder. Biological Psychiatry, 72(6), 448-456.

Herman, J. L. (2015). Trauma and recovery: The aftermath of violence--From domestic abuse to political terror. Basic Books.

Hoffman, P. D., & Fruzzetti, A. E. (2007). Advances in interventions for families with a relative with a personality disorder diagnosis. Current Opinion in Psychiatry, 20(1), 13-18.

Hoffman, P. D., Fruzzetti, A. E., Buteau, E., Neiditch, E. R., Penney, D., Bruce, M. L., ... & Struening, E. (2005). Family connections: A program for relatives of persons with borderline personality disorder. Family Process, 44(2), 217-225.

Hooley, J. M., & Gotlib, I. H. (2000). A diathesis-stress conceptualization of expressed emotion and clinical outcome. Applied and Preventive Psychology, 9(3), 135-151.

Hooley, J. M., & Hoffman, P. D. (1999). Expressed emotion and clinical outcome in borderline personality disorder. American Journal of Psychiatry, 156(10), 1557-1562.

Kreisman, J. J., & Straus, H. (2010). Sometimes I act crazy: Living with borderline personality disorder. John Wiley & Sons.

Linehan, M. M. (2014). DBT Skills training manual (2nd ed.). Guilford Publications.

Meaney-Tavares, R., & Haseley, D. (2019). Safe enough spaces: A psychoanalytic perspective on sanctuary trauma. Psychoanalytic Social Work, 26(1), 1-18.

Paris, J. (2019). Treatment of borderline personality disorder: A guide to evidence-based practice (2nd ed.). Guilford Press.

Paris, J. (2020). Stepped care for borderline personality disorder: Making treatment accessible. Academic Press.

Pearlin, L. I., Mullan, J. T., Semple, S. J., & Skaff, M. M. (1990). Caregiving and the stress process: An overview of concepts and their measures. The Gerontologist, 30(5), 583-594.

Rnic, K., Dozois, D. J., & Martin, R. A. (2018). Cognitive distortions, humor styles, and depression. Europe's Journal of Psychology, 14(3), 632-650.

Schulze, L., Schmahl, C., & Niedtfeld, I. (2016). Neural correlates of disturbed emotion processing in borderline personality disorder: A multimodal meta-analysis. Biological Psychiatry, 79(2), 97-106.

Sherry, S. B., Gautreau, C. M., Mushquash, A. R., Sherry, D. L., & Allen, S. L. (2014). Self-critical perfectionism confers vulnerability to depression after controlling for neuroticism: A longitudinal study of middle-aged, community-dwelling women. Personality and Individual Differences, 69, 1-4.

Ulrich, R., Bogren, L., Gardiner, S., & Lundin, S. (2018). Psychiatric ward design can reduce aggressive behavior. Journal of Environmental Psychology, 57, 53-66.

van der Kolk, B. A. (2014). The body keeps the score: Brain, mind, and body in the healing of trauma. Viking.(see the generated image above)

Walsh, F. (2016). Strengthening family resilience (3rd ed.). Guilford Publications.

Zanarini, M. C. (2009). Psychotherapy of borderline personality disorder. Acta Psychiatrica Scandinavica, 120(5), 373-377.

Zanarini, M. C., Frankenburg, F. R., Hennen, J., Reich, D. B., & Silk, K. R. (2007). Prediction of the 10-year course of borderline personality disorder. American Journal of Psychiatry, 164(5), 827-832.

Zanarini, M. C., Frankenburg, F. R., Reich, D. B., & Fitzmaurice, G. (2010). Time to attainment of recovery from borderline personality disorder and stability of recovery: A 10-year prospective follow-up study. American Journal of Psychiatry, 167(6), 663-667.

Zanarini, M. C., Frankenburg, F. R., Reich, D. B., Wedig, M. M., Conkey, L. C., & Fitzmaurice, G. M. (2018). The course of marriage/sustained cohabitation and parenthood among borderline patients followed prospectively for 20 years. Journal of Personality Disorders, 32(6), 737-750.

Zimmerman, M., Rothschild, L., & Chelminski, I. (2005). The prevalence of DSM-IV personality disorders in psychiatric outpatients. American Journal of Psychiatry, 162(10), 1911-1918.